Polynesia

by David Zurick

foreword by Alan Marcus

SHANTI ARTS PUBLISHING
BRUNSWICK, MAINE

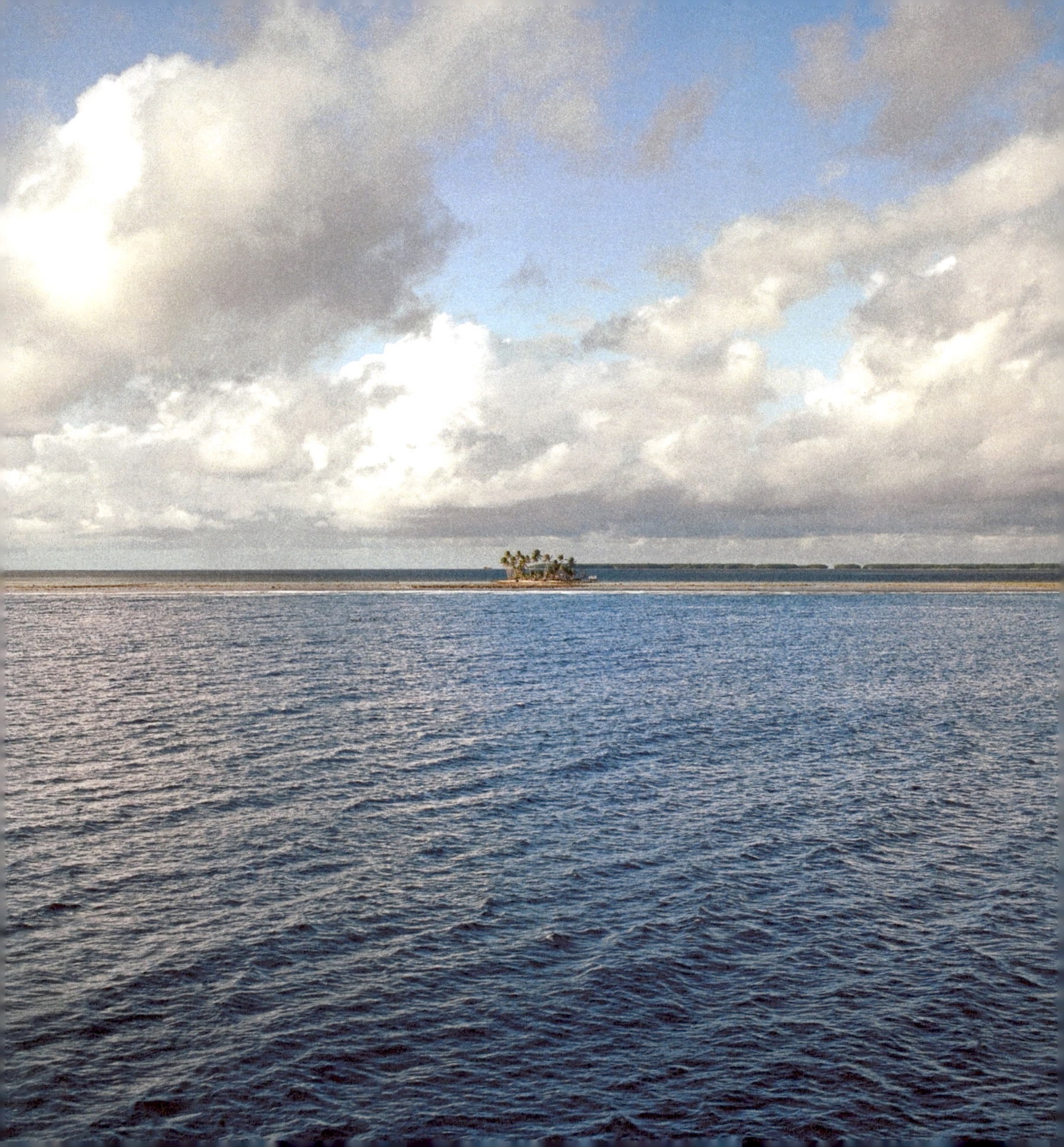

Foreword

When first we glance at and then study the photographs captured by David Zurick's camera, two aspects become apparent. Each image is framed with precision and care, offering a momentary portal of a place and time. The featured sky and seascape or rock formation are imbued with a seemingly timeless character. Thus, the photographs in this collection invite us to consider a place where beauty and time find harmony. Yet, in their juxtaposition with one another, paradoxes emerge around society's impact on the natural environment. As the book's narrative progresses, we are made to confront the challenges of contested land use and the implications of urbanization. The smiles and facial queries that address us, signal that these Pacific islands do not exist in a naturalistic void, but rather are places where humans thrive and are in need of accommodation. These images serve to diversify our engagement with tropical island settings by displaying their variations and hues. Whether encouraging romanticized or more forthright interpretations, they also challenge our own fixation with consumption and cultural appropriation. Having met in Honolulu and traveled parallel paths in Samoa and other Pacific islands, I recognize within David Zurick's work ecosystems which appear in balance and others which face uncertainty due to human needs and desires. His visual artistry mesmerizes but does not obscure. The fusion of land, sea and air illustrate a tranquility that exists within his frame and for us to imagine or to find in our discovery of the places themselves. Through the alchemy of his informed vision, we are invited to voyage and to pay witness.

—Alan Marcus, Professor and Chair of Visual Culture
University of Aberdeen

The loveliest fleet of islands that lie anchored in any ocean.

— Mark Twain

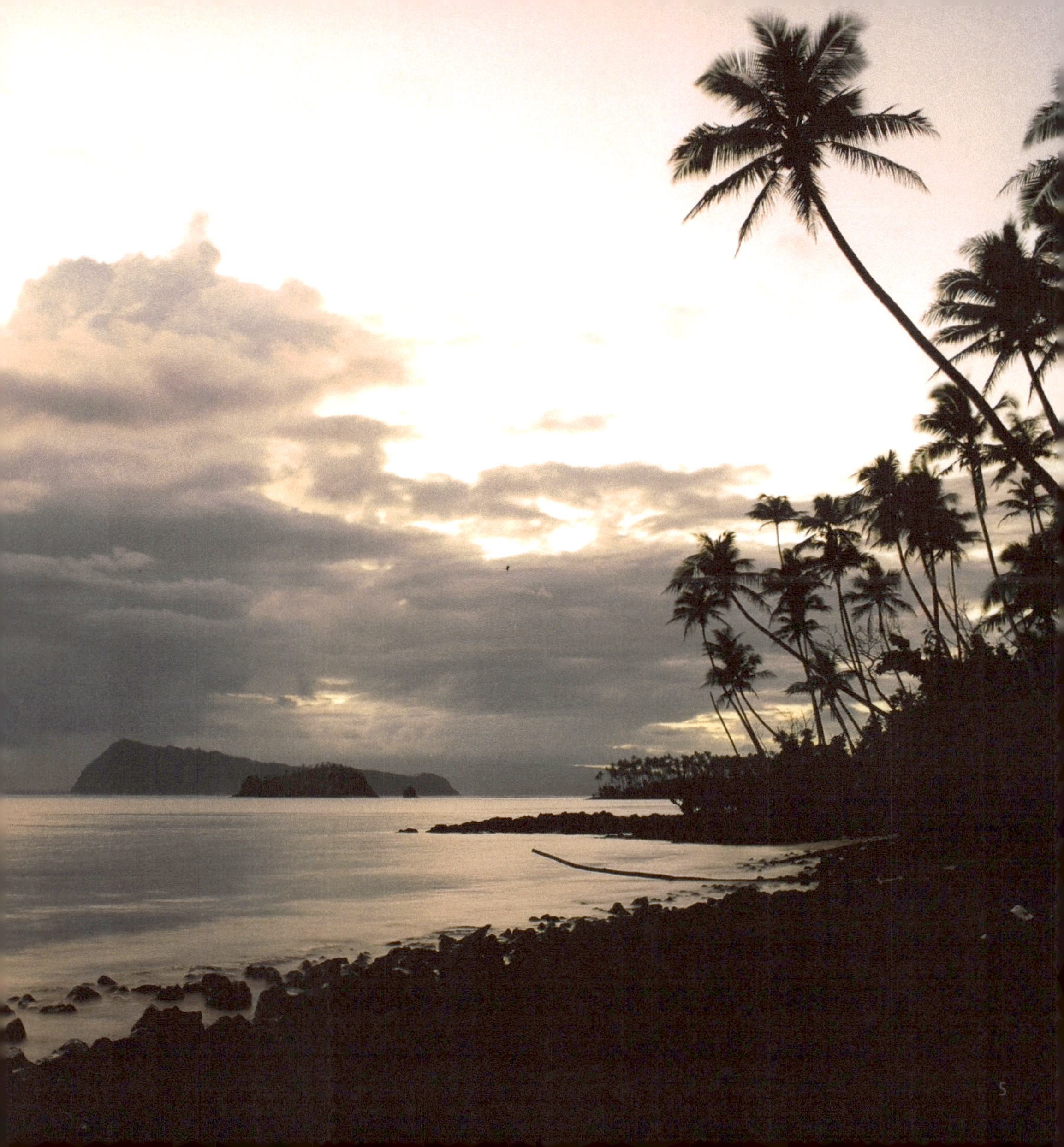

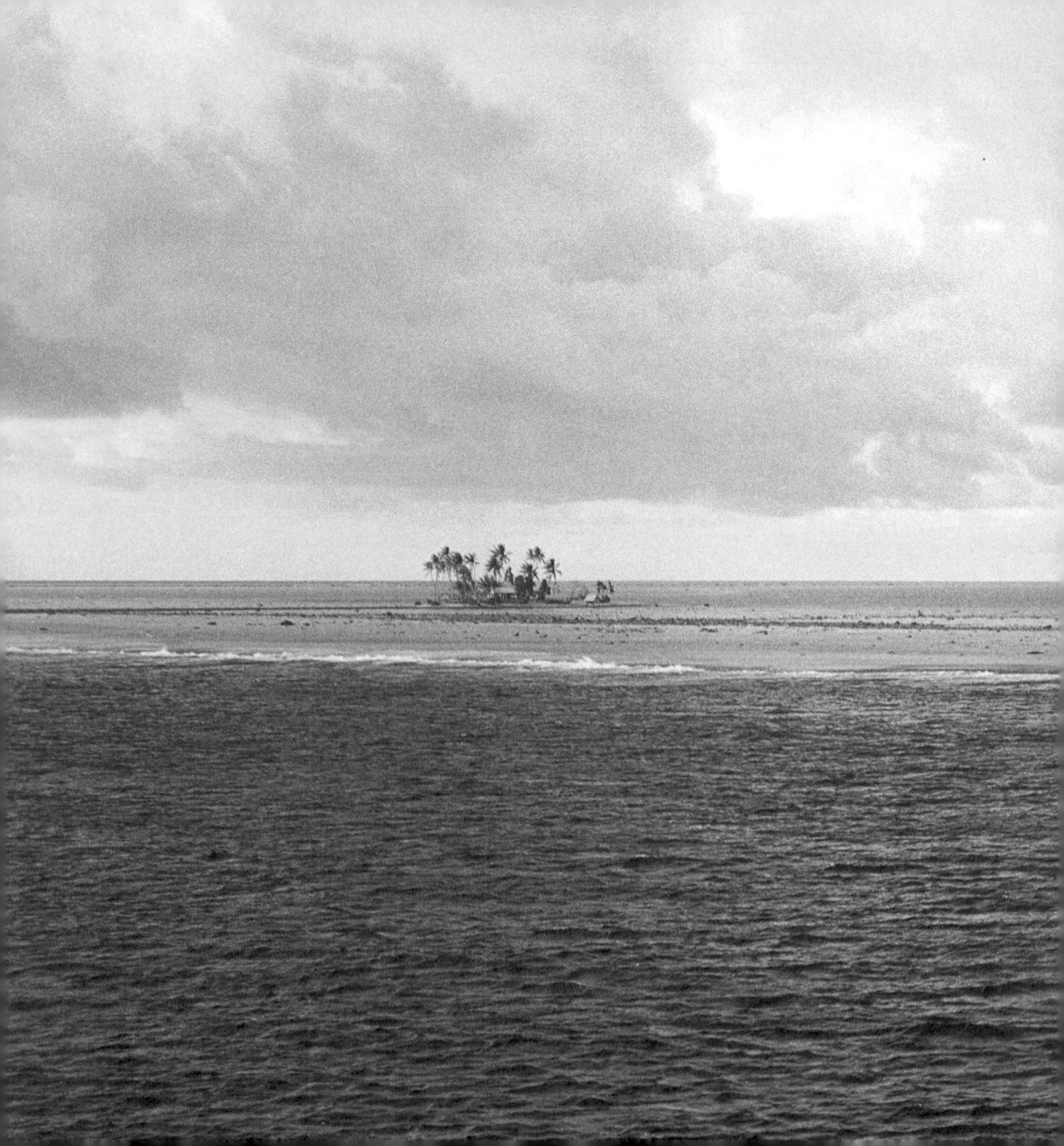

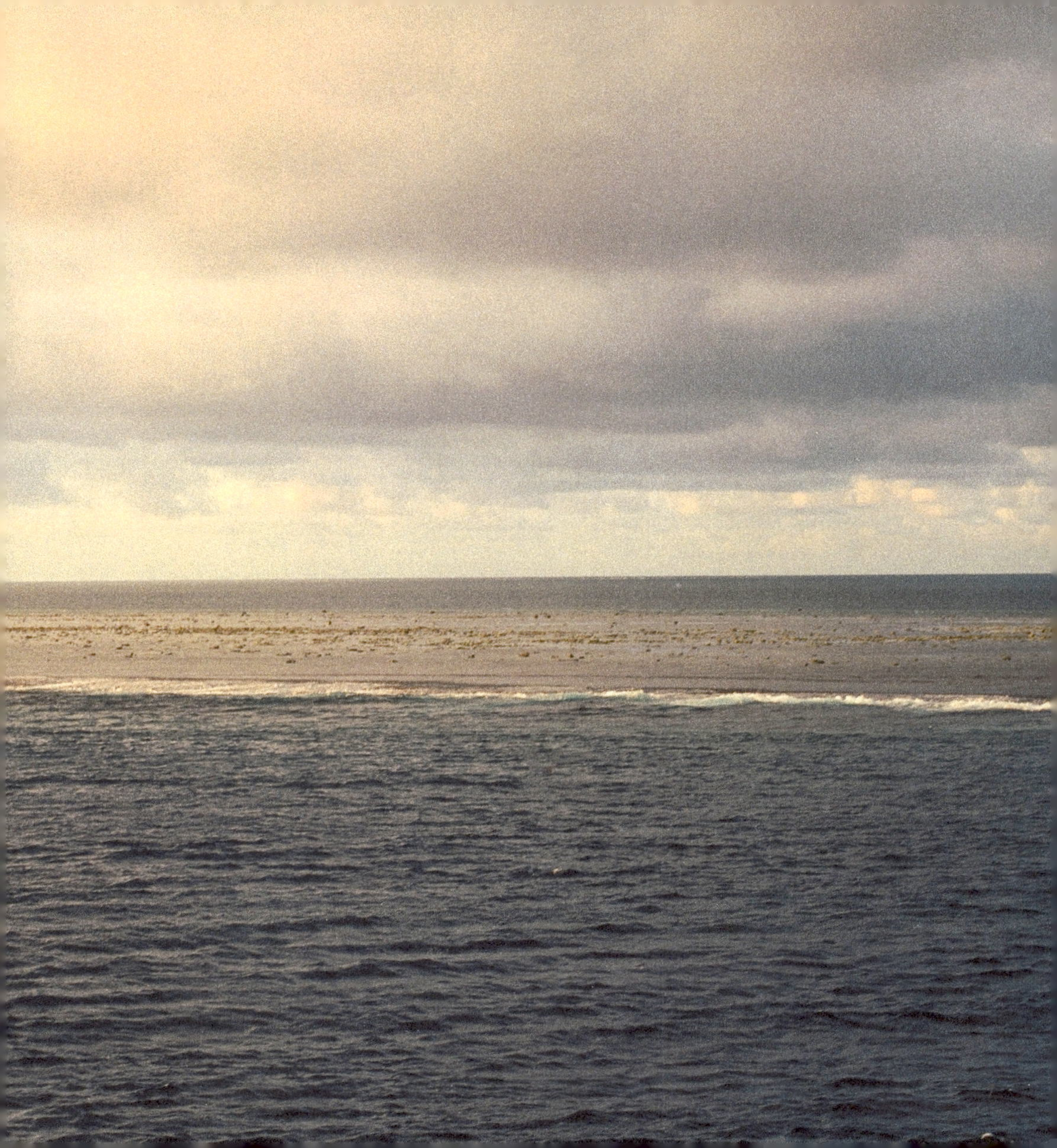

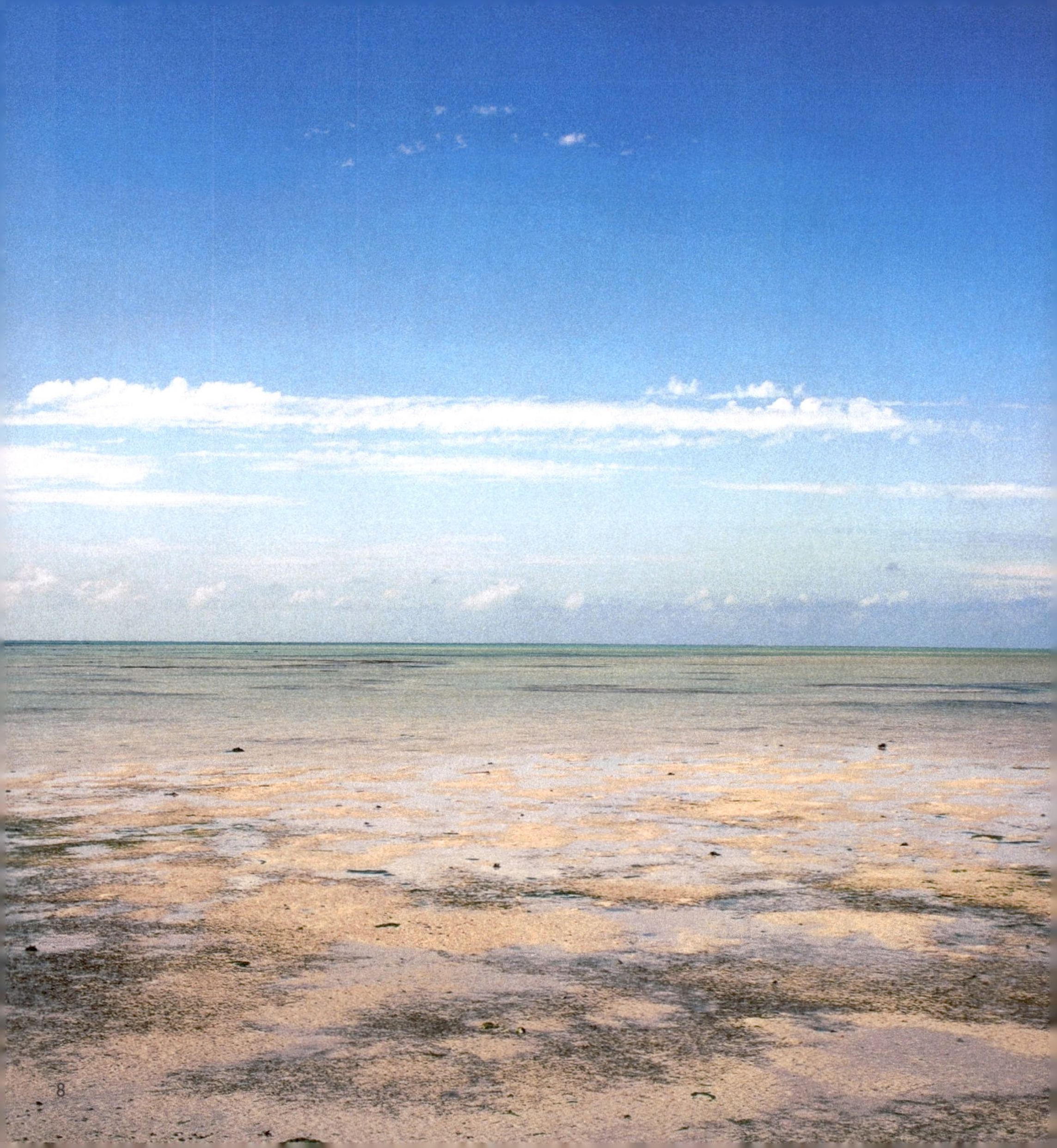

Sea and Sky

Polynesia appears on a map as a widely-spaced group of more than one thousand islets flung across 800,000 square miles of Pacific Ocean. It was while voyaging from Samoa to Tokelau on a bimonthly run of the cargo vessel Wairua that I was able to see past the numbers to gain a fuller sense of this vast oceanic realm. We'd been at sea for several days, and in all directions the horizon split the world into shimmering hemispheres of air and water. The ocean appeared boundless. When the tiny coral atolls of Faka'ofo appeared before my ship, I saw them as improbable slivers of palm-fringed greenery wedged between sea and sky. It was hard to imagine people living on them, yet they have been inhabited for one thousand years.

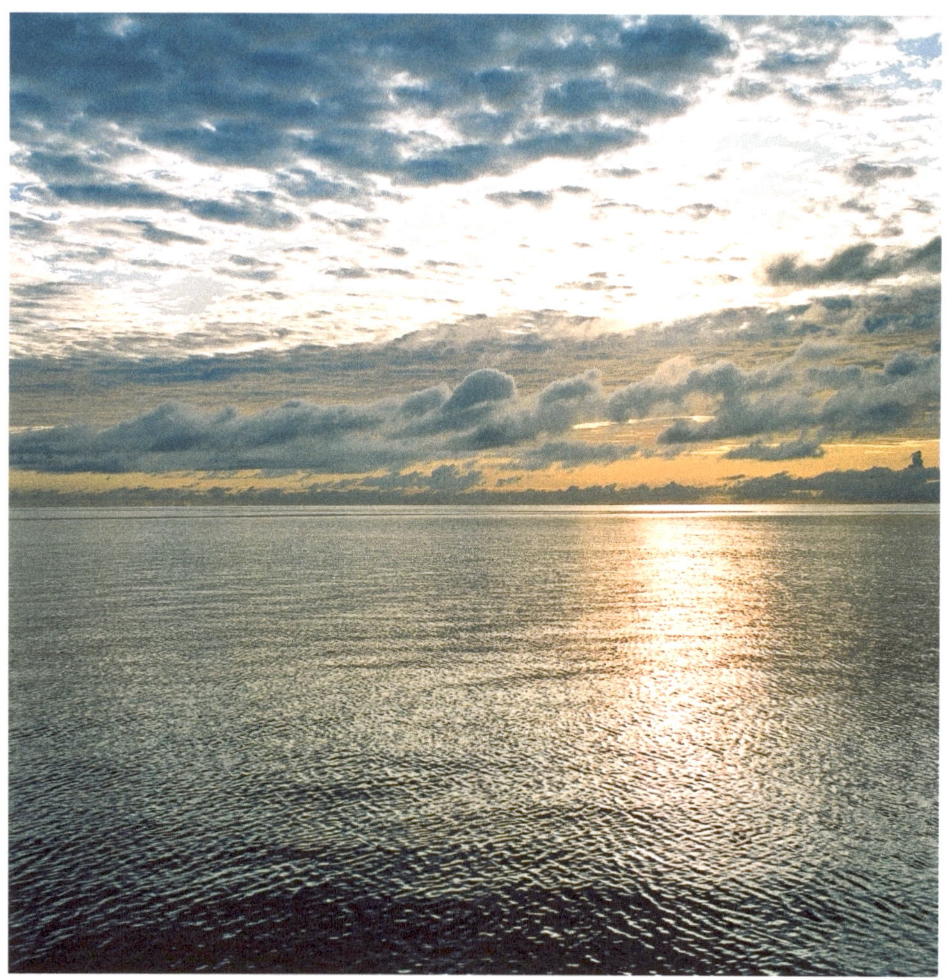

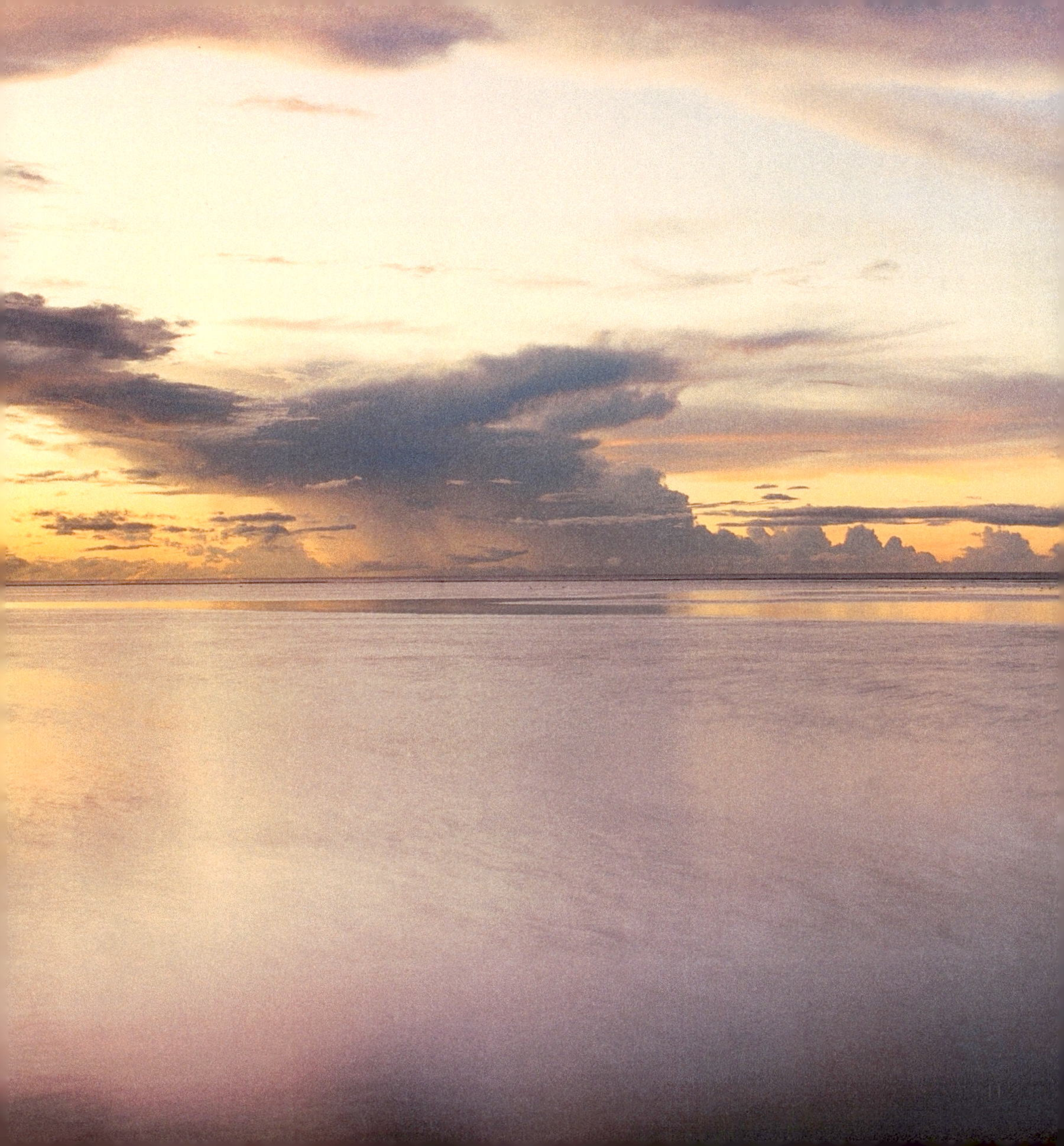

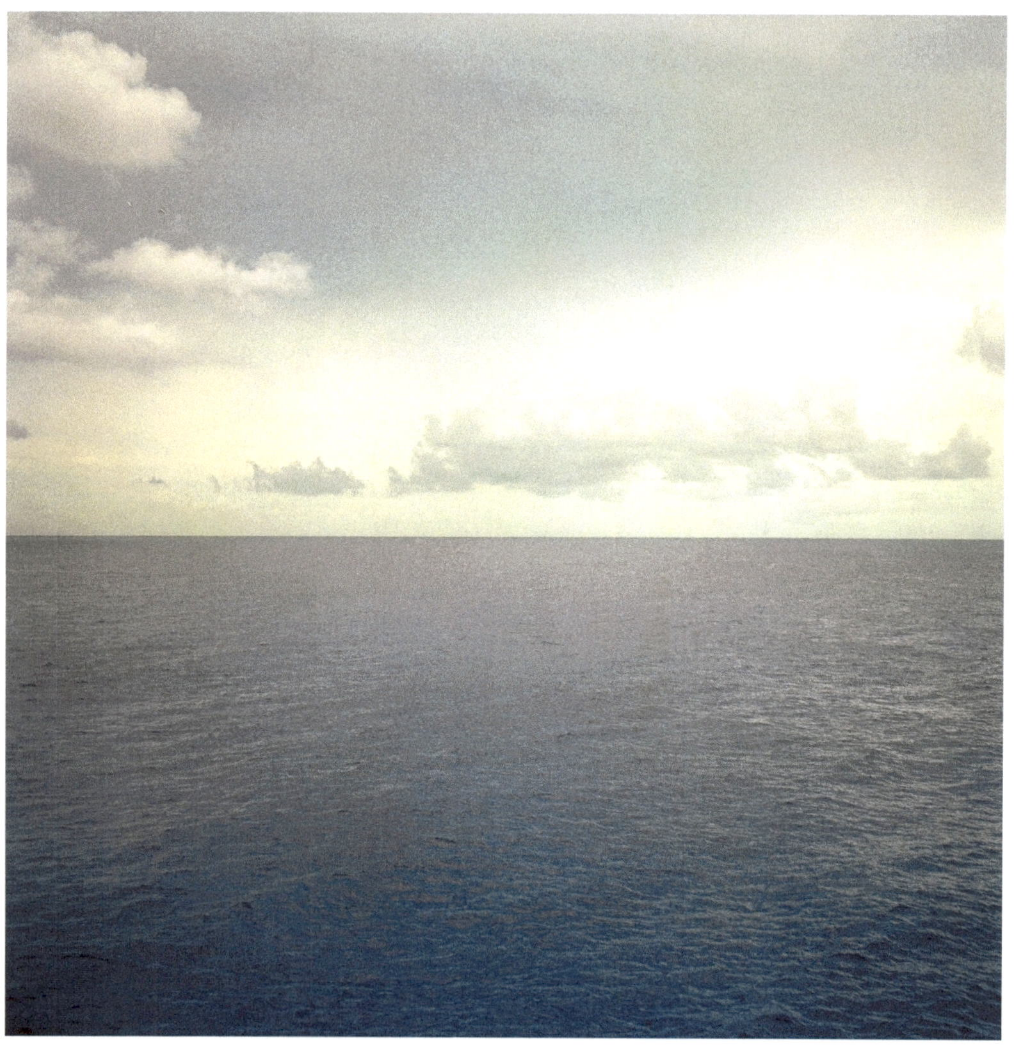

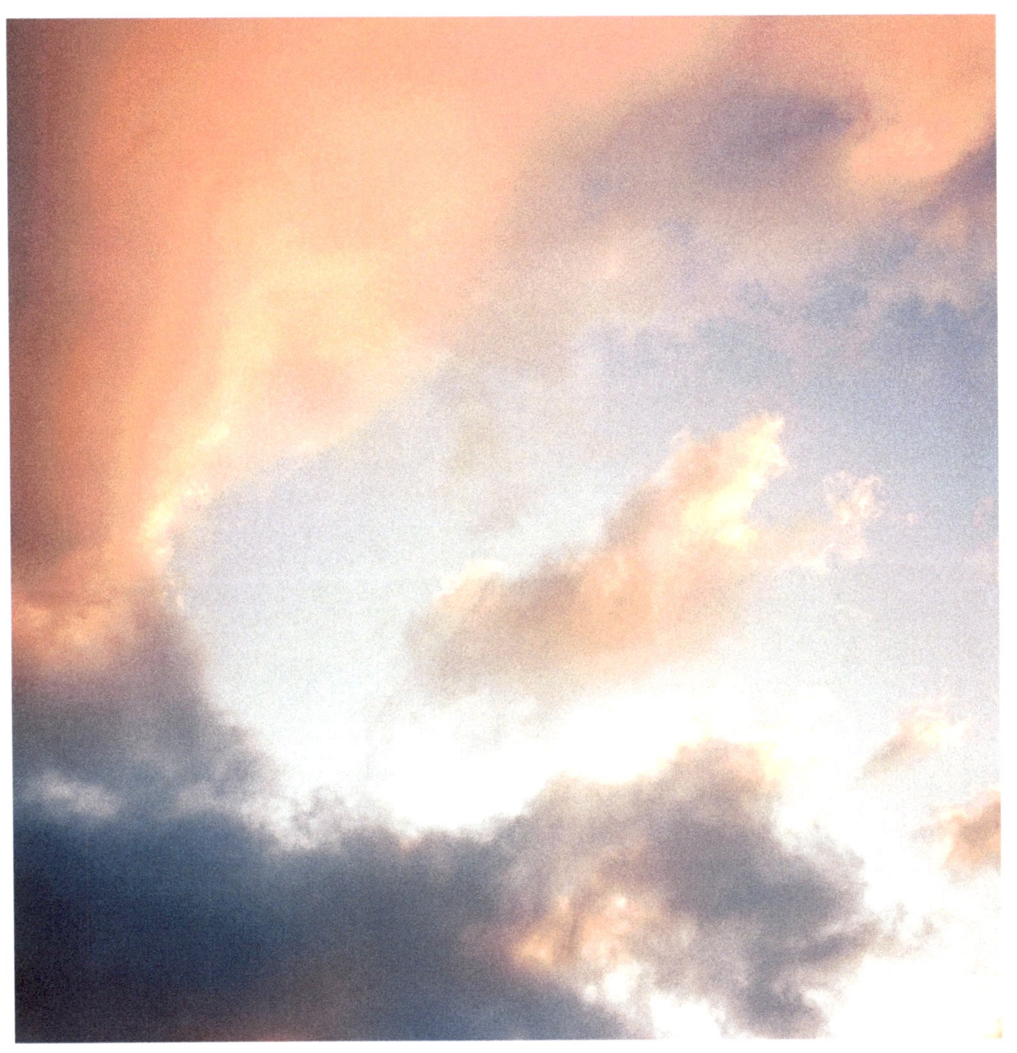

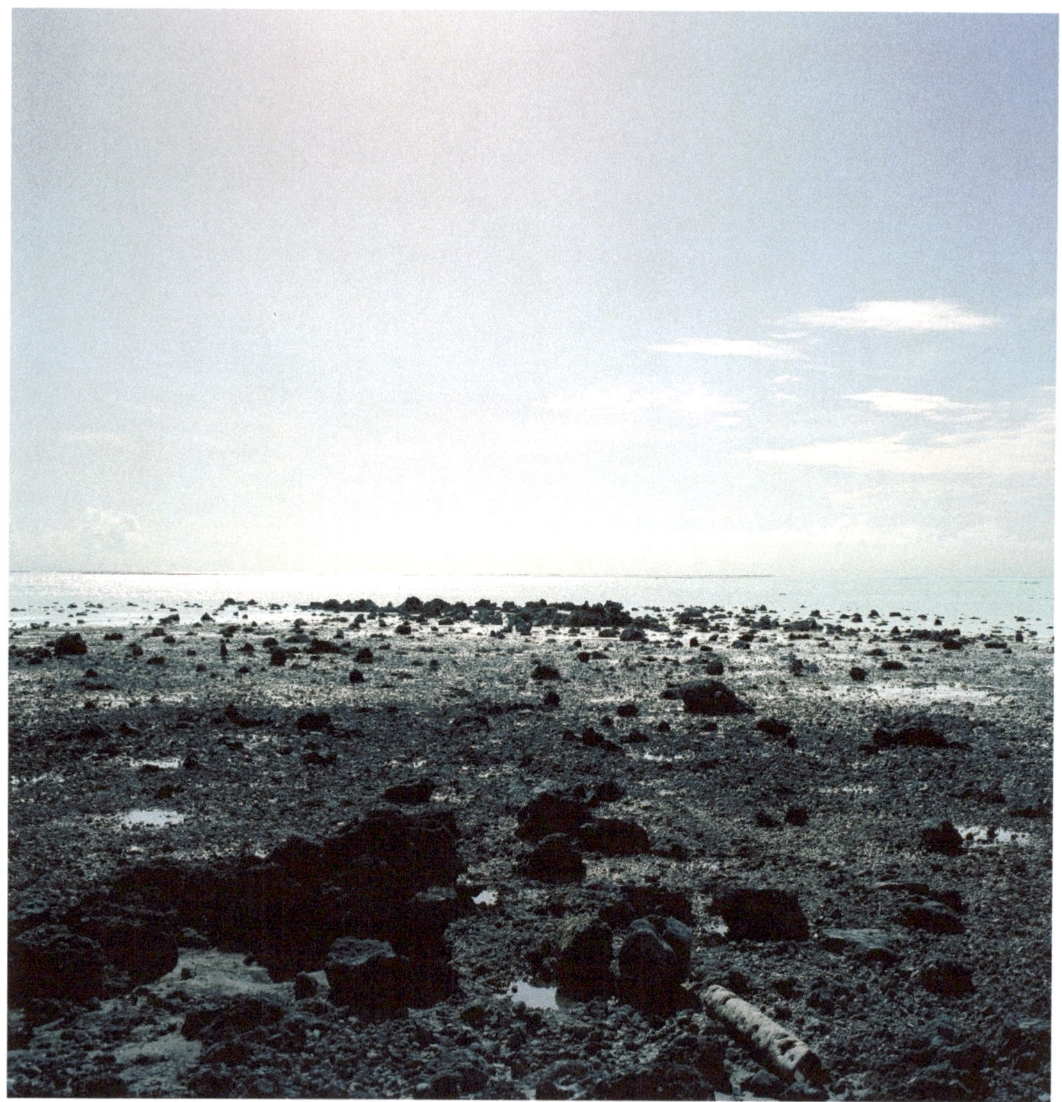

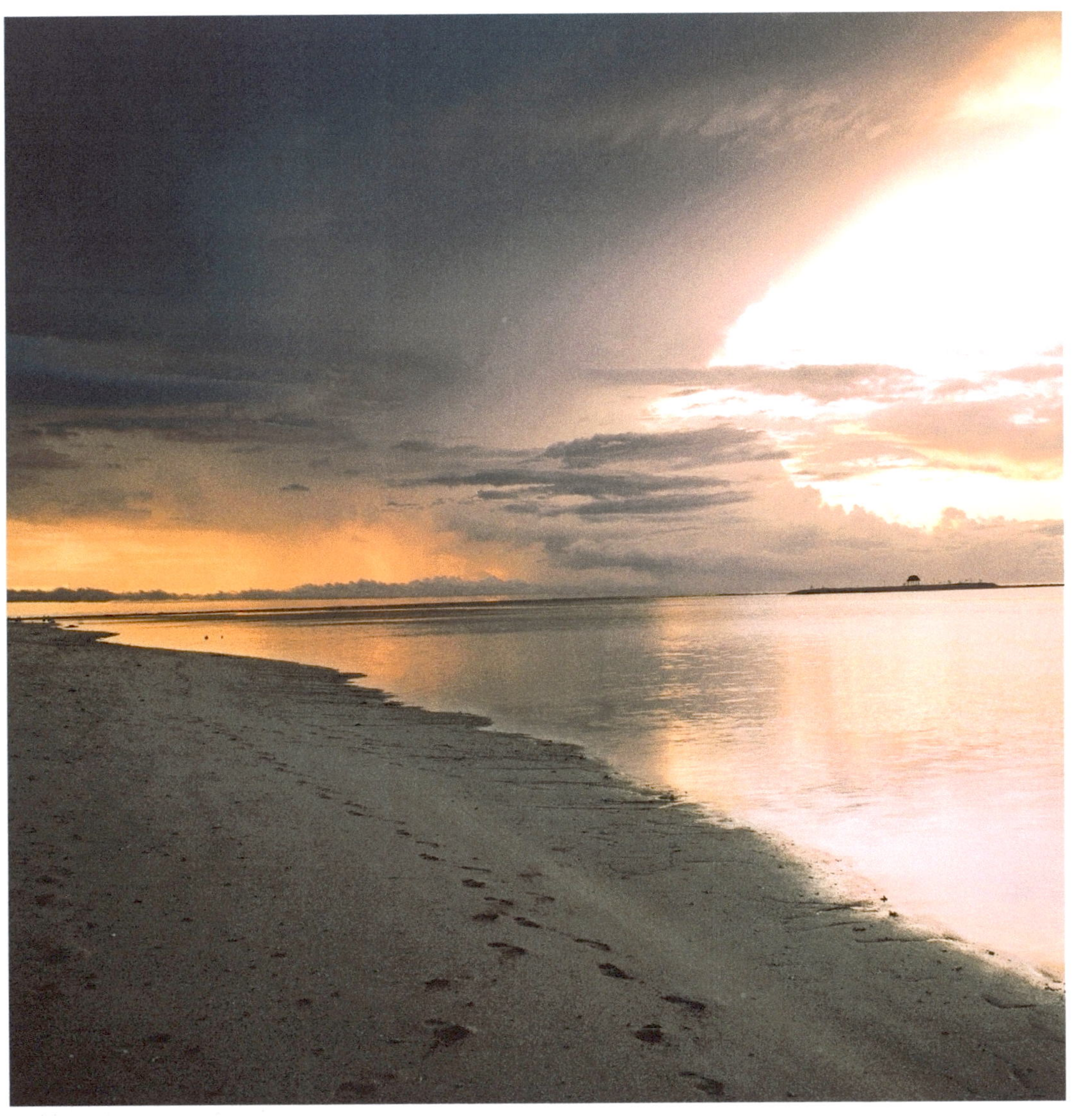

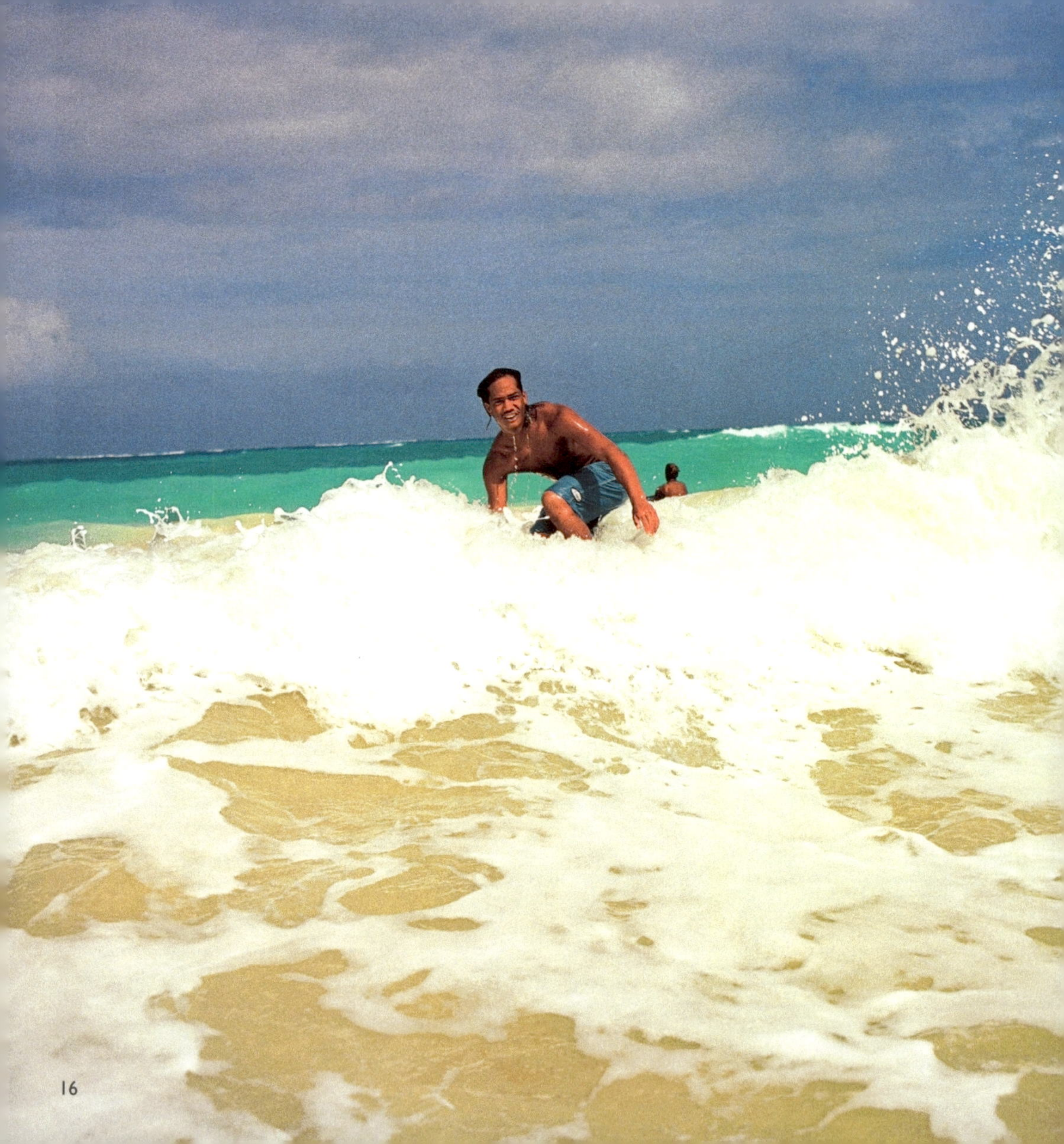

Our water is so full of life; it's the fastest water in the world. That's all there is to it.

— Duke Kahanamoku

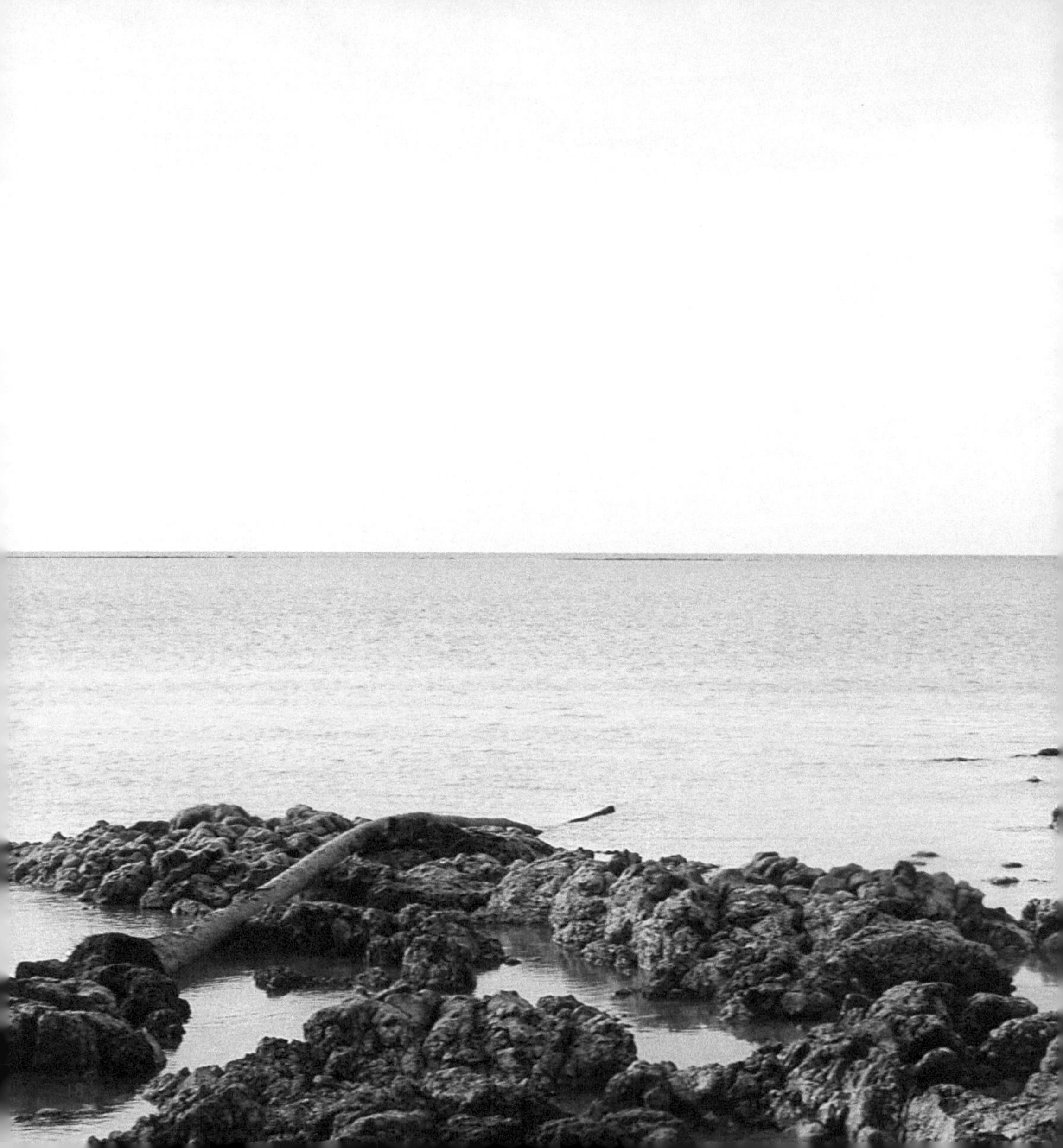

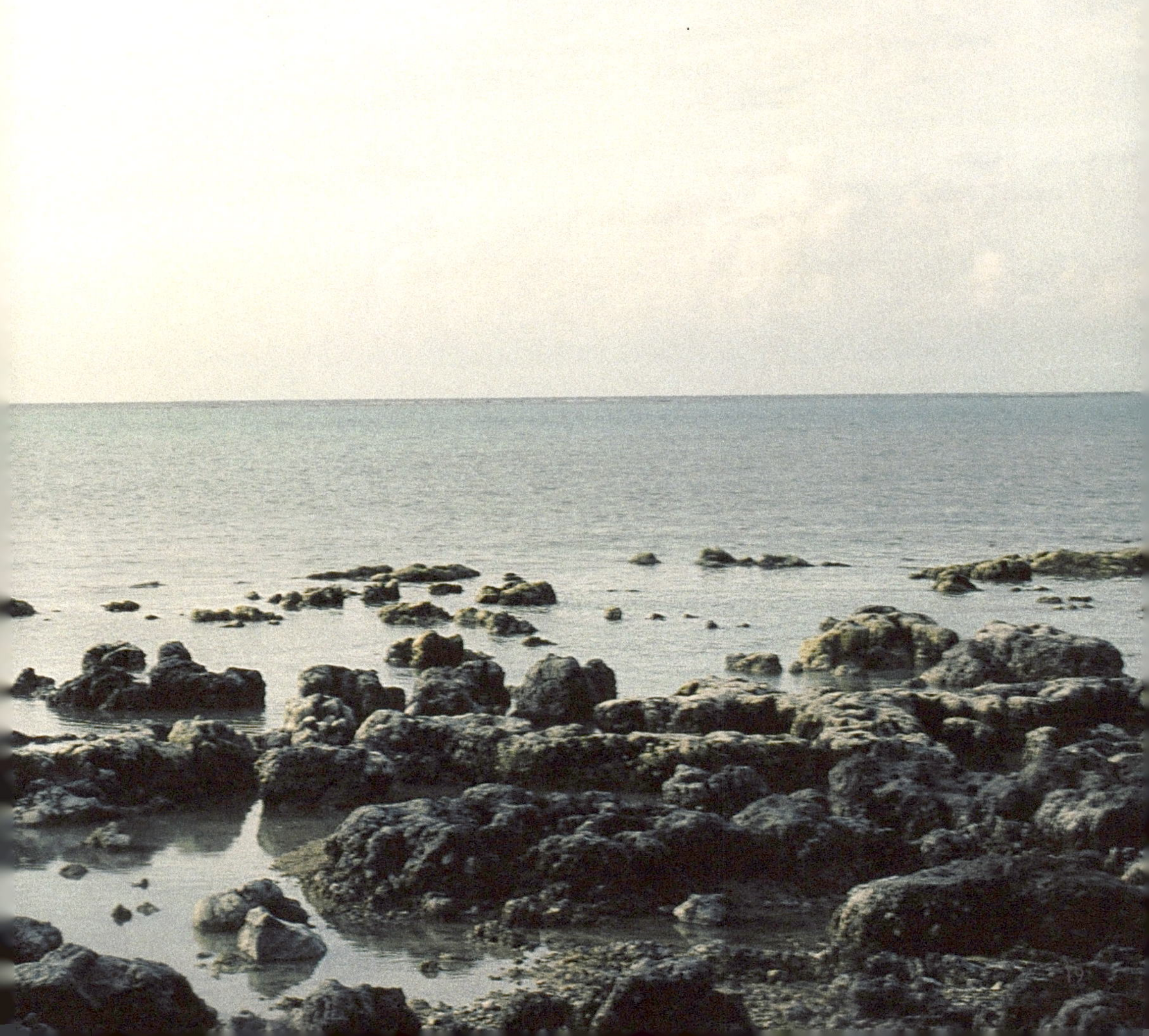

Volcanoes in the Ocean

The Polynesian islands are the eroded remnants of volcanoes rising from the ocean floor. Over time, rain, wind, and waves have carved their land surfaces into innumerable sizes and shapes, from Tokelau's low-lying atolls, where the maximum elevation is fifteen feet above sea level, to the summit of Hawaii (Mauna Kea) at 13,803 feet. In a spectacular way, the life-cycle of a Polynesian island can be witnessed on the island of Hawaii, where ongoing eruptions from the Kilauea volcano pour rivers of magma into the ocean. There, I watched glowing lava enter the cool water amid billowing clouds of vapor and gases and immediately disintegrate into sand particles. Earth's newest beach was taking shape in front of me.

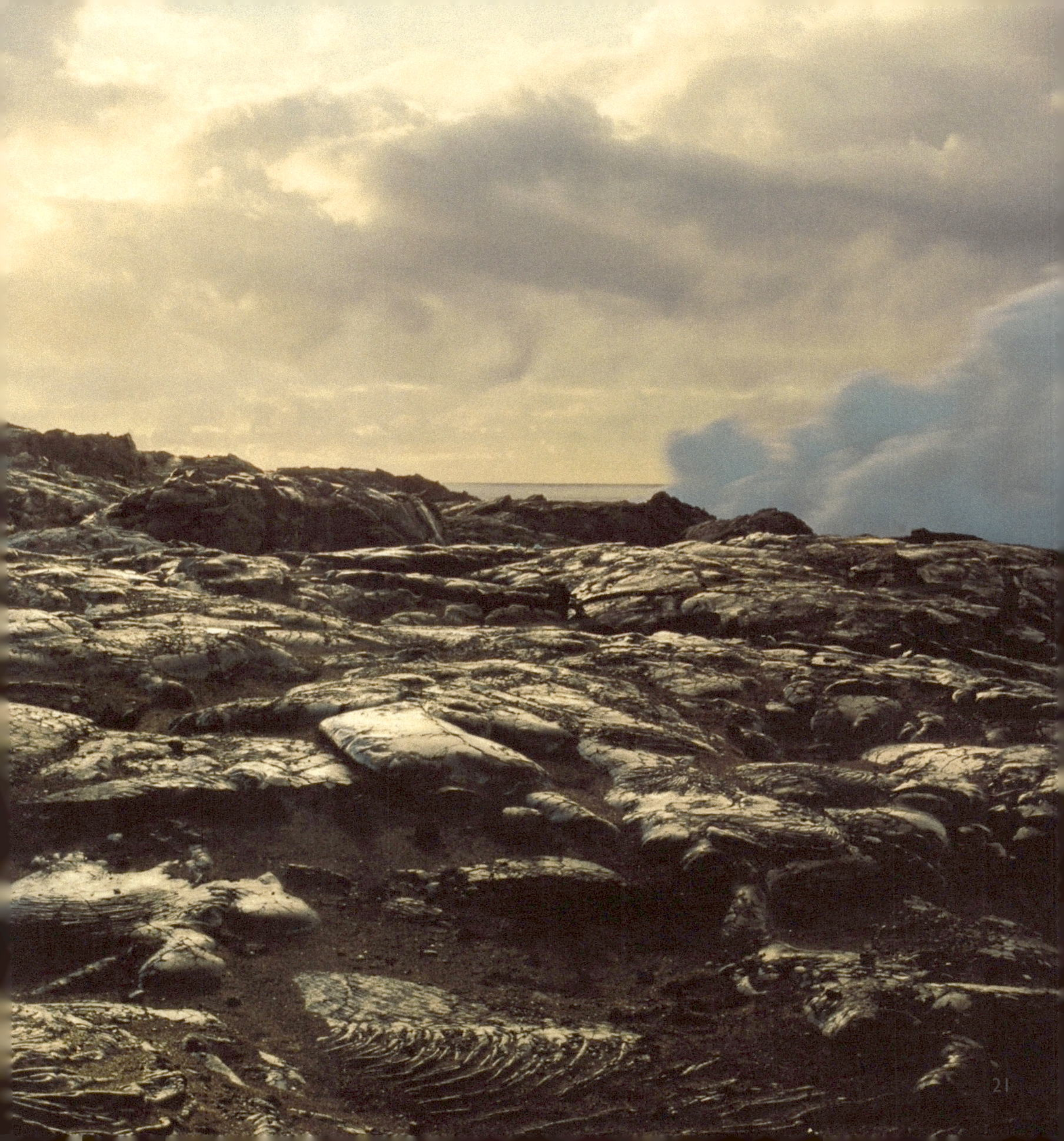

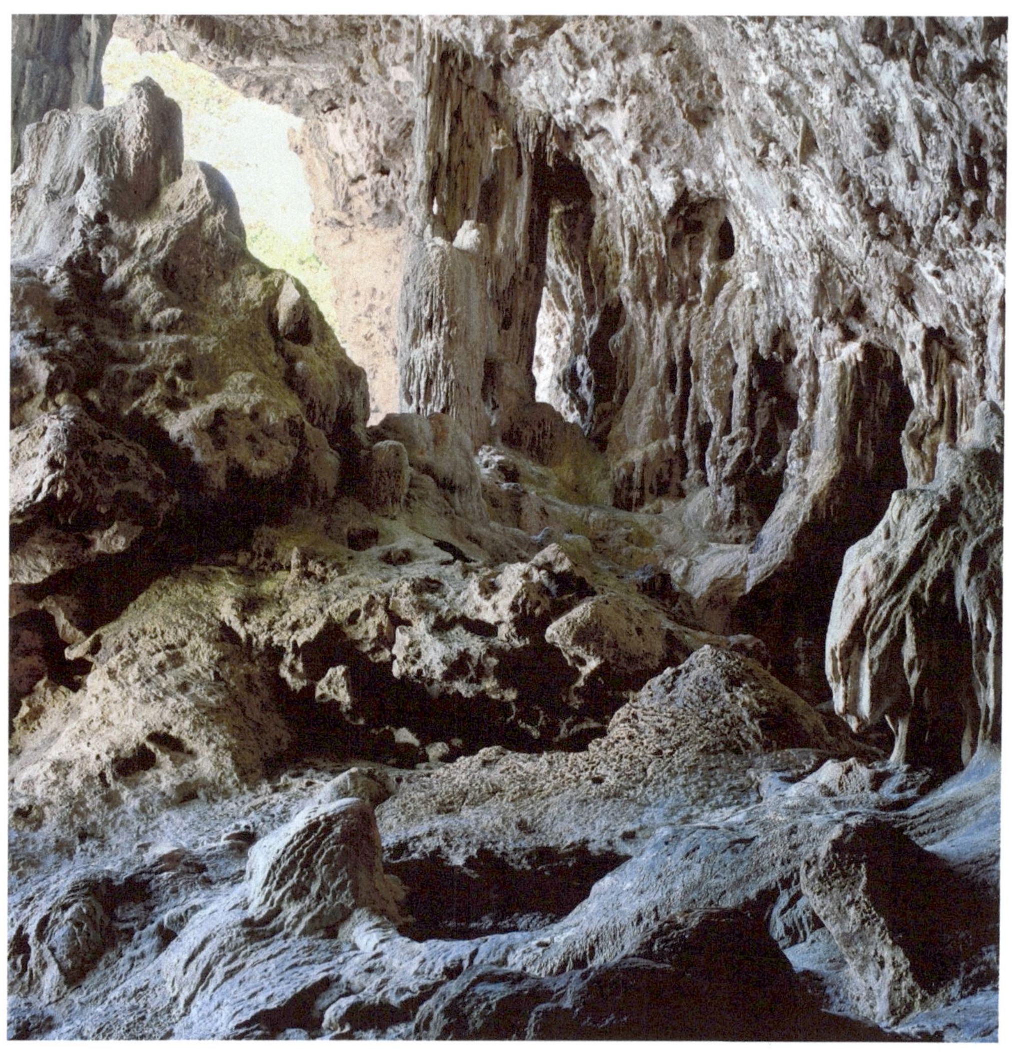

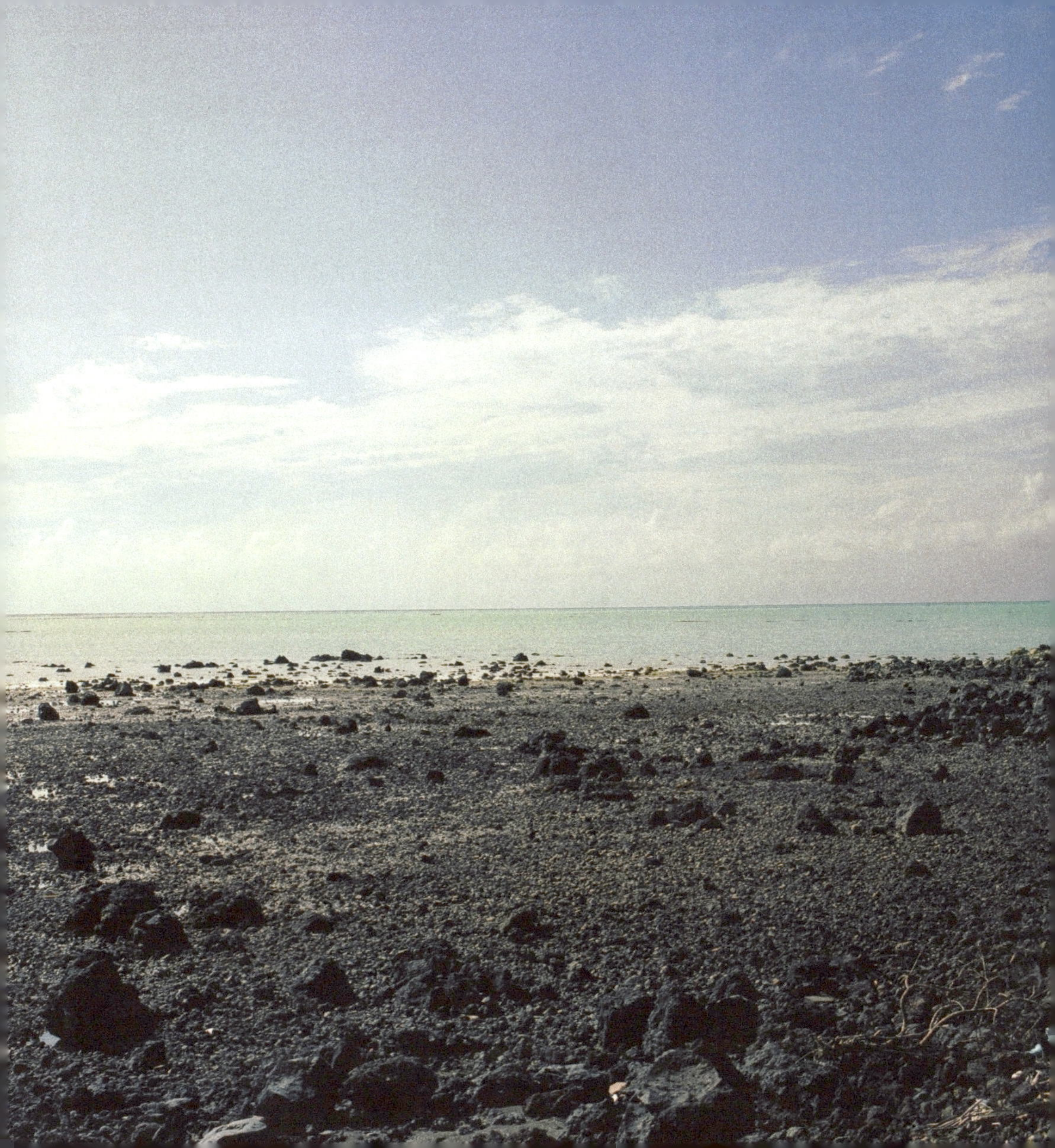

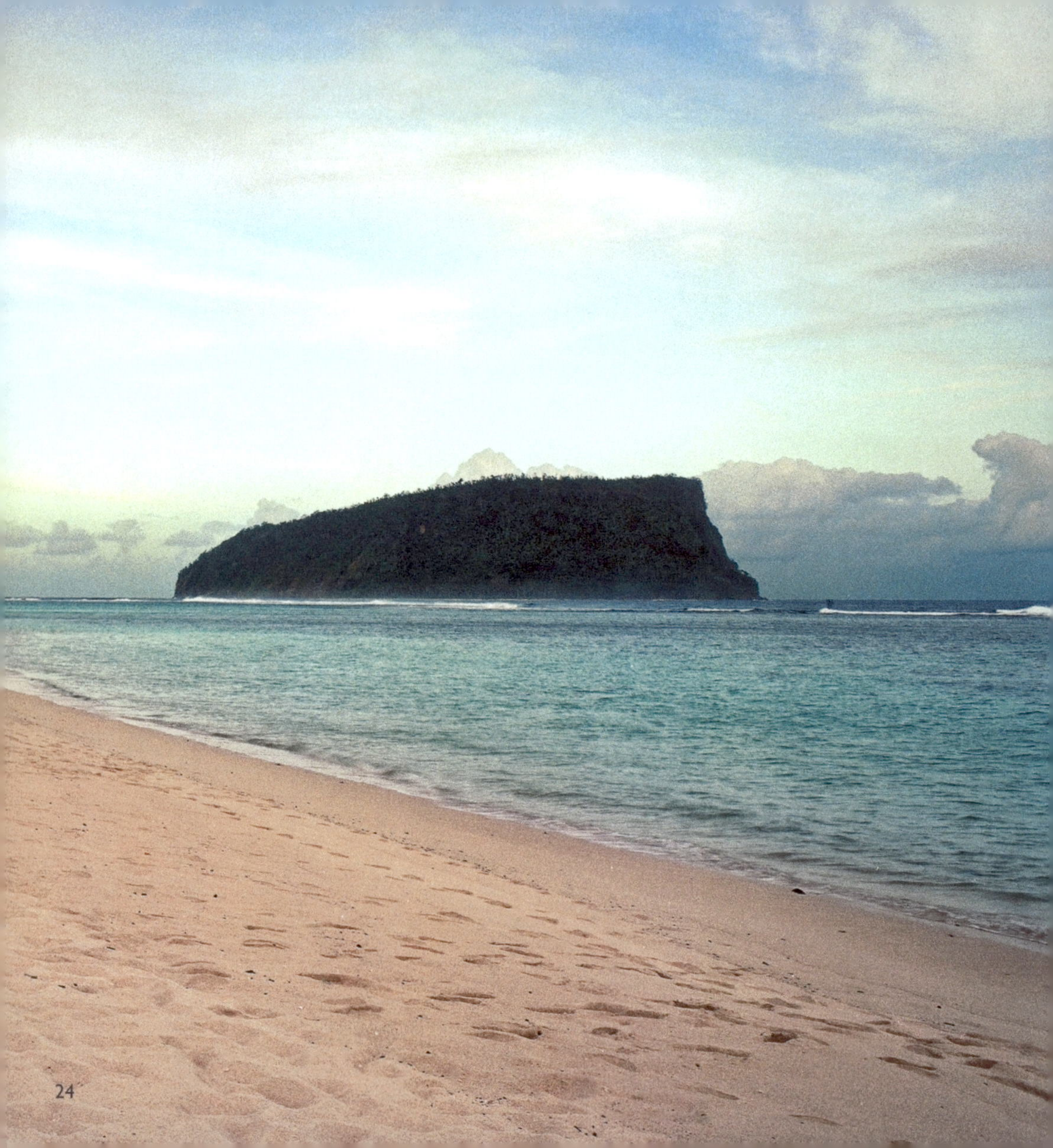

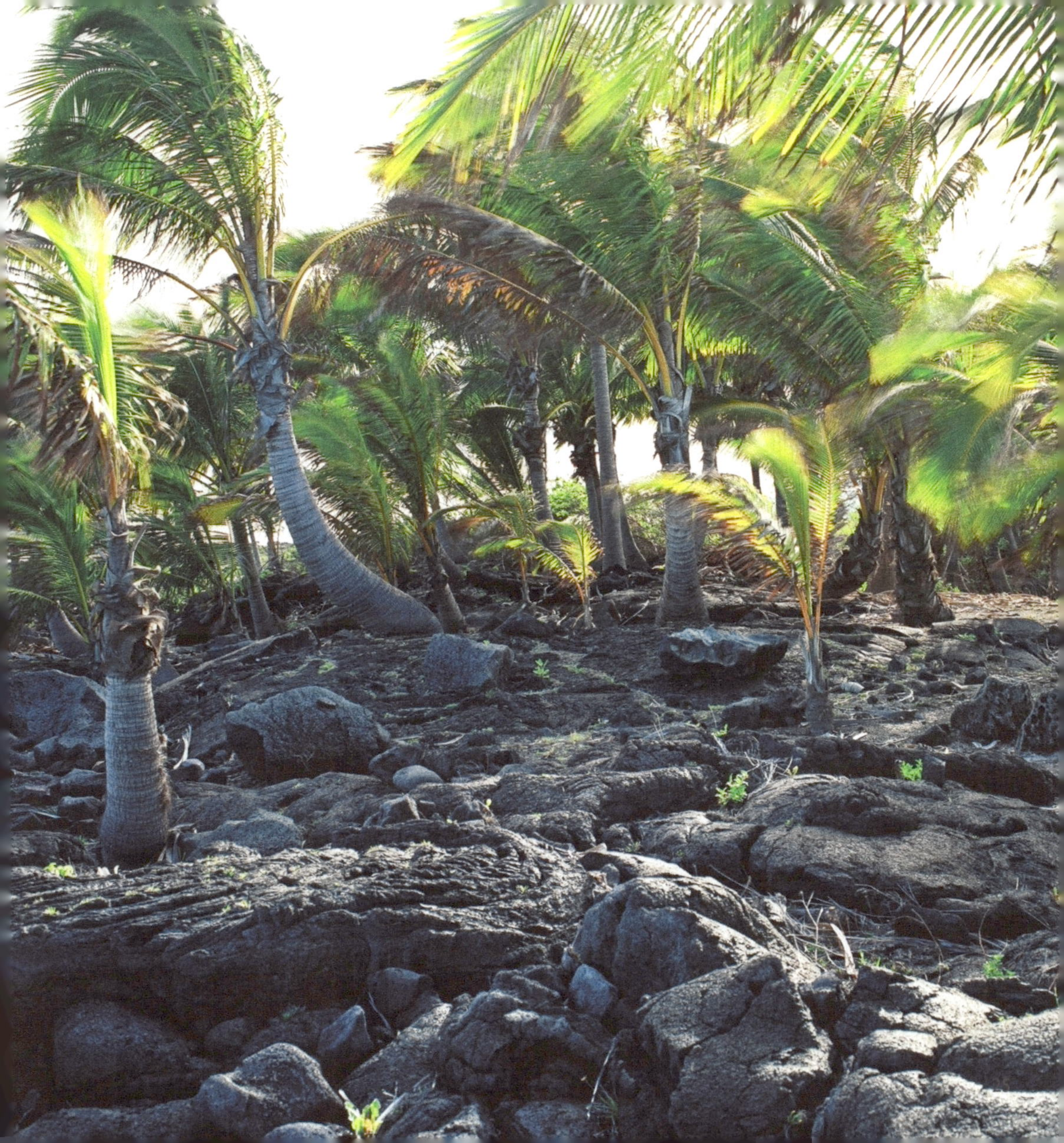

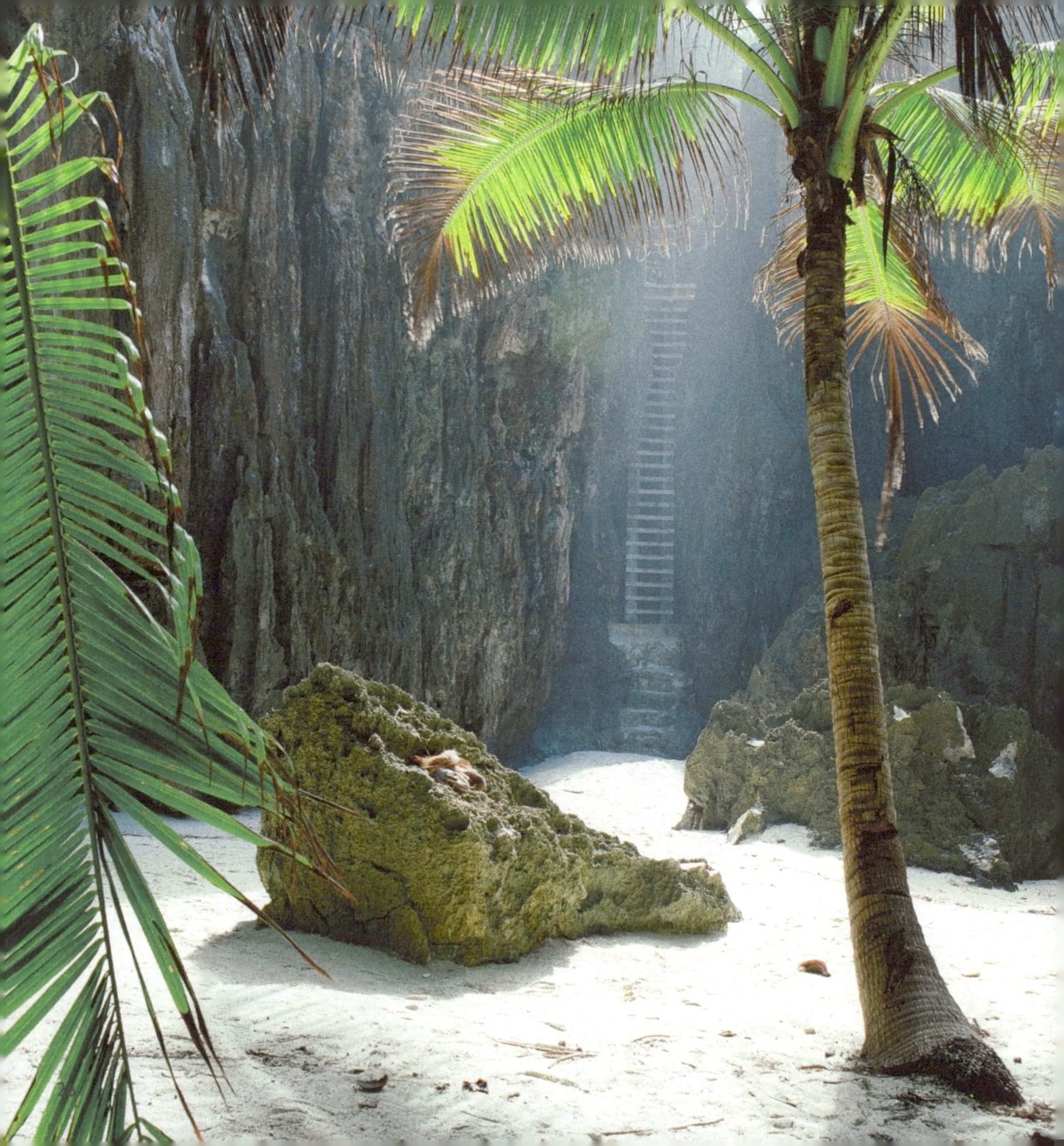

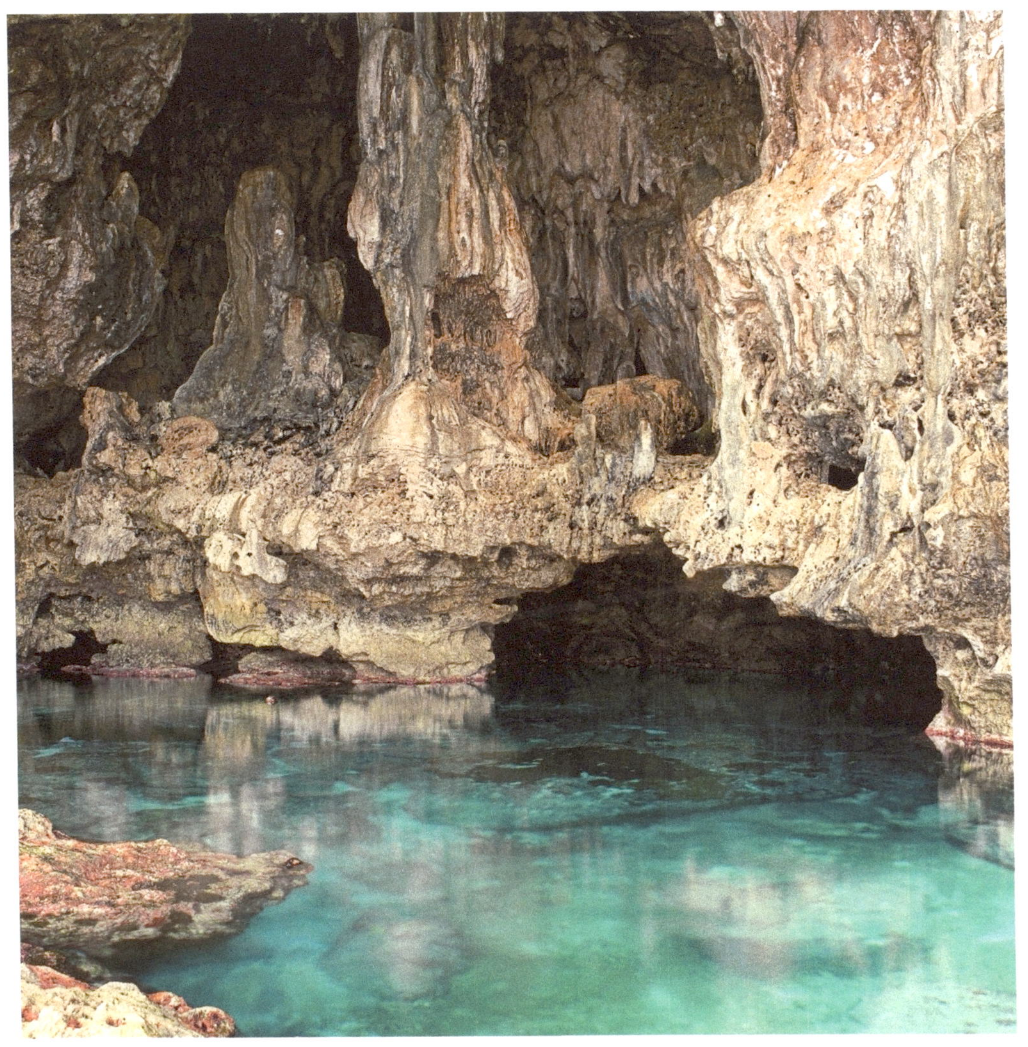

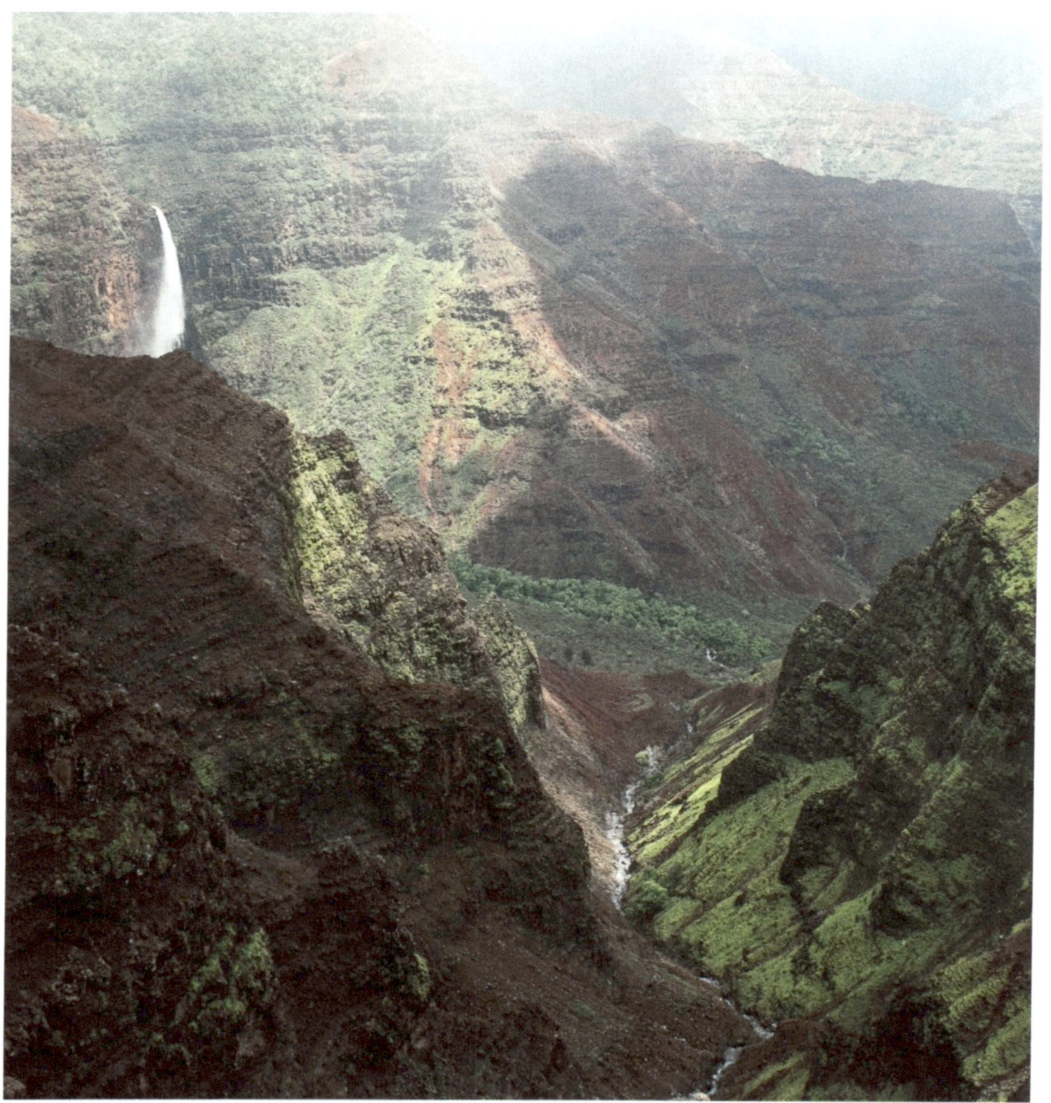

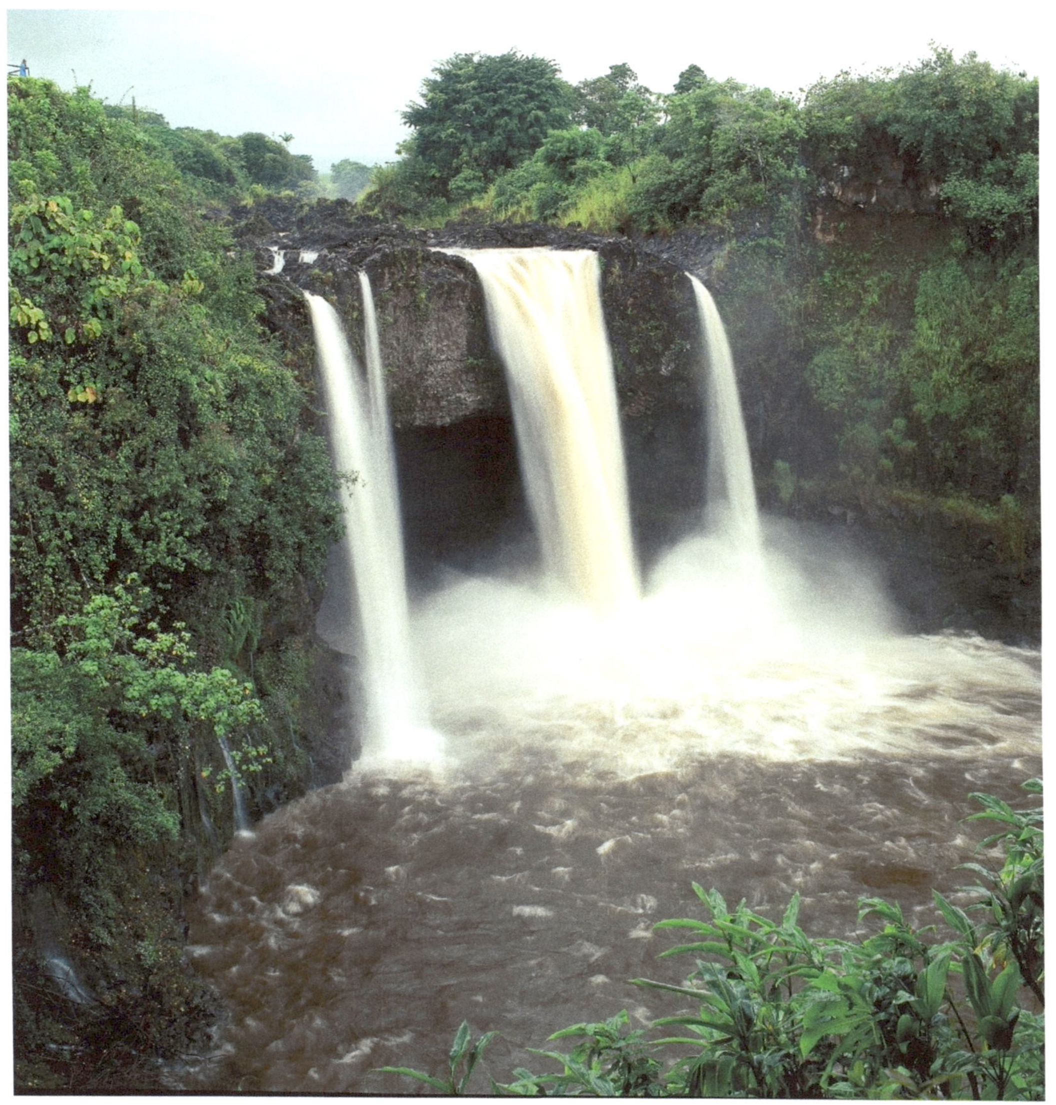

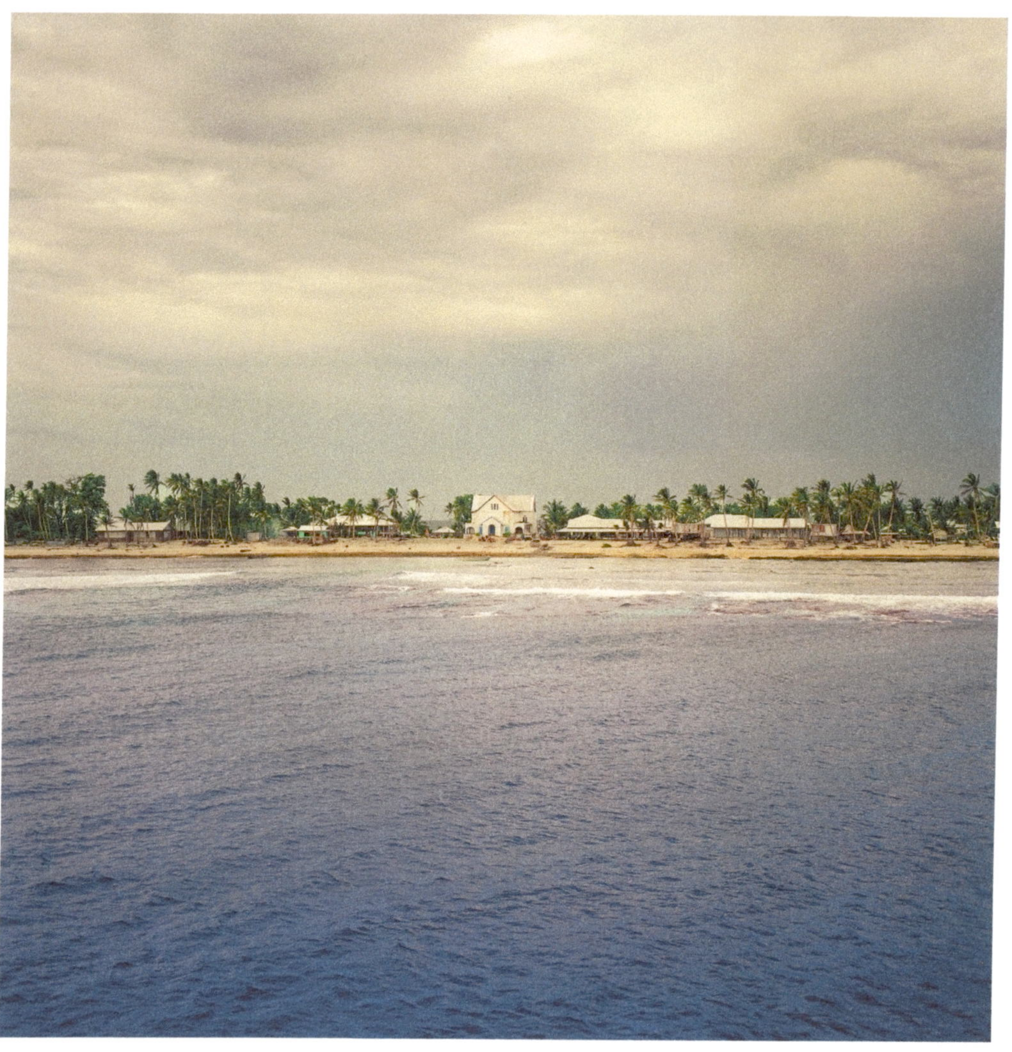

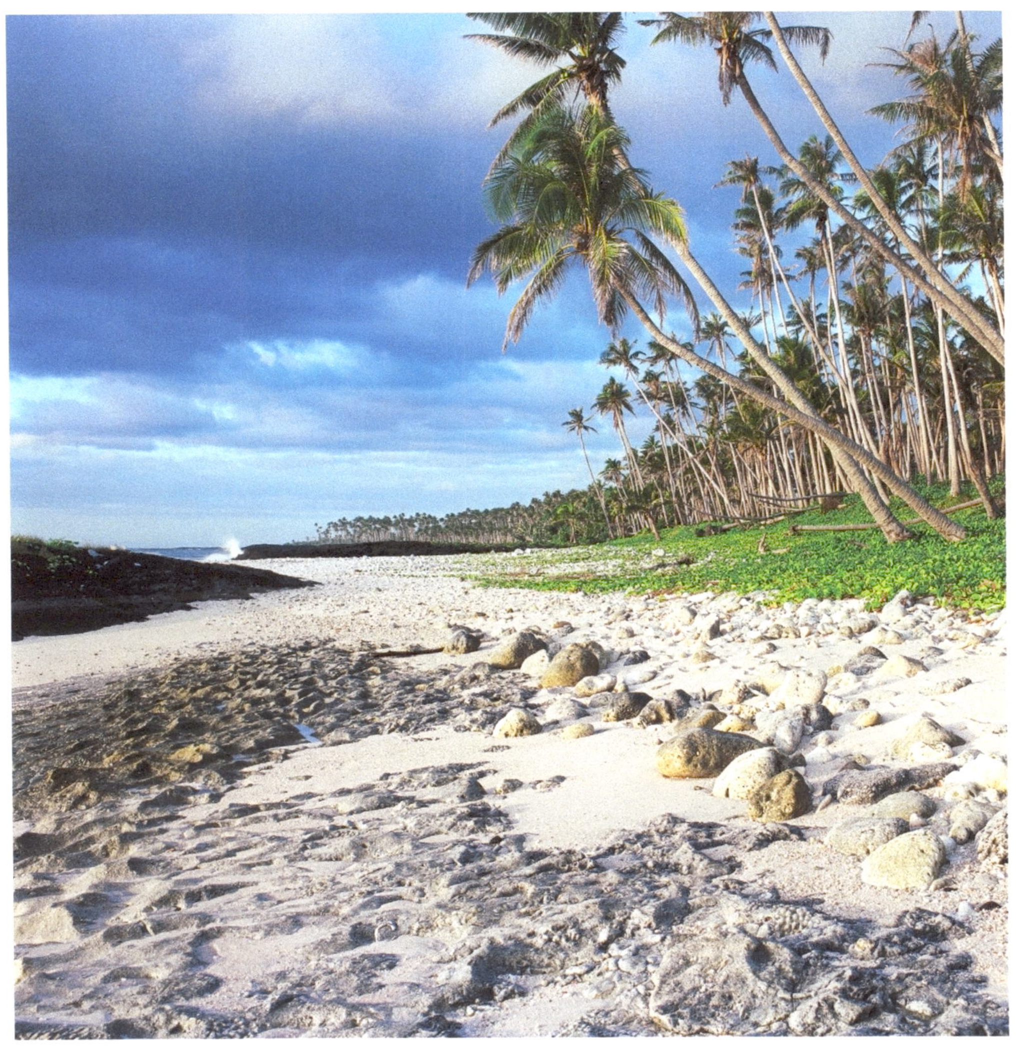

Jets of lava gushed from Kahiki. Pele hurled her lightning,
vomit of flame, outpouring of lava was the woman's farewell.

—Traditional Hawaiian chant

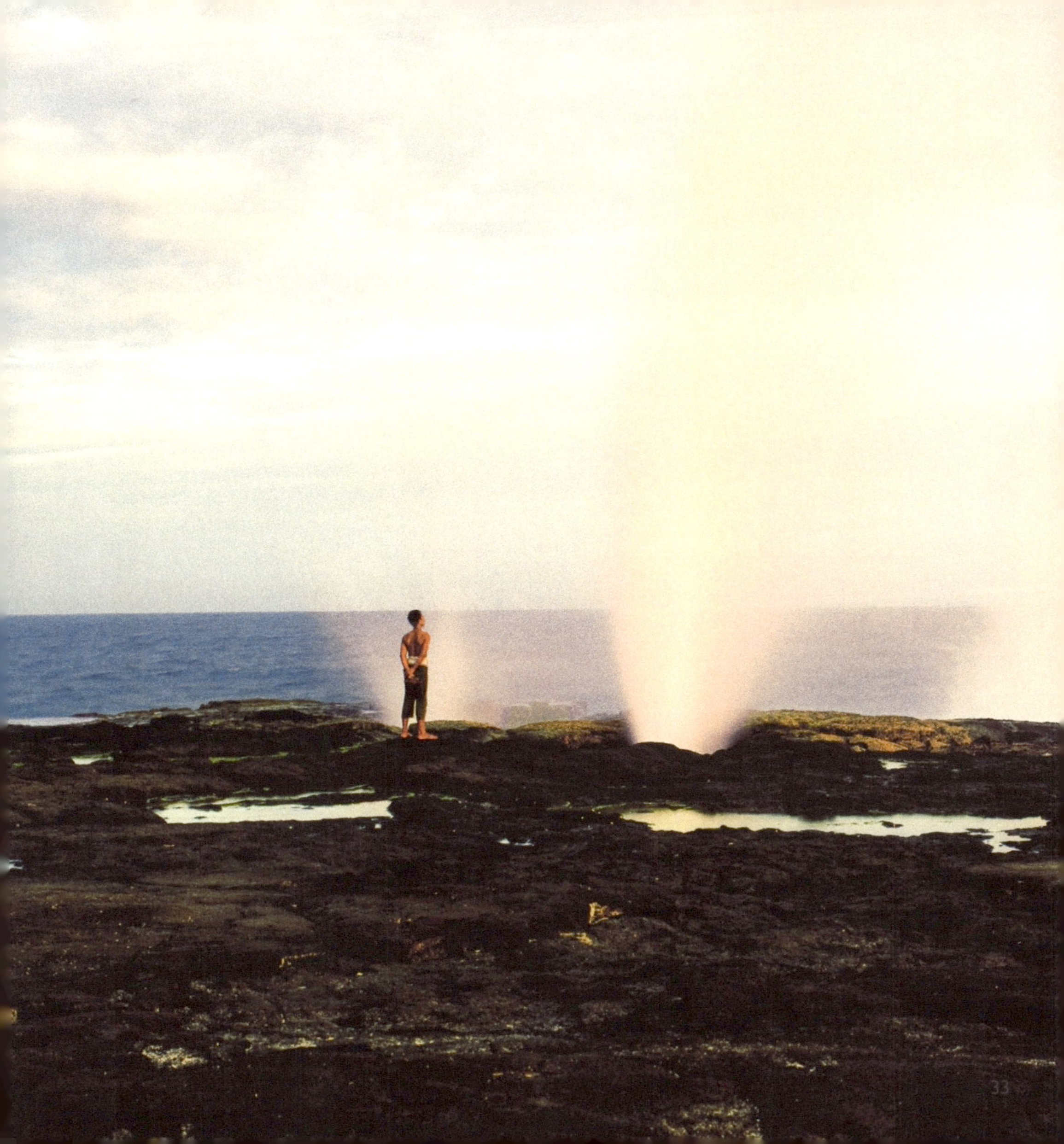

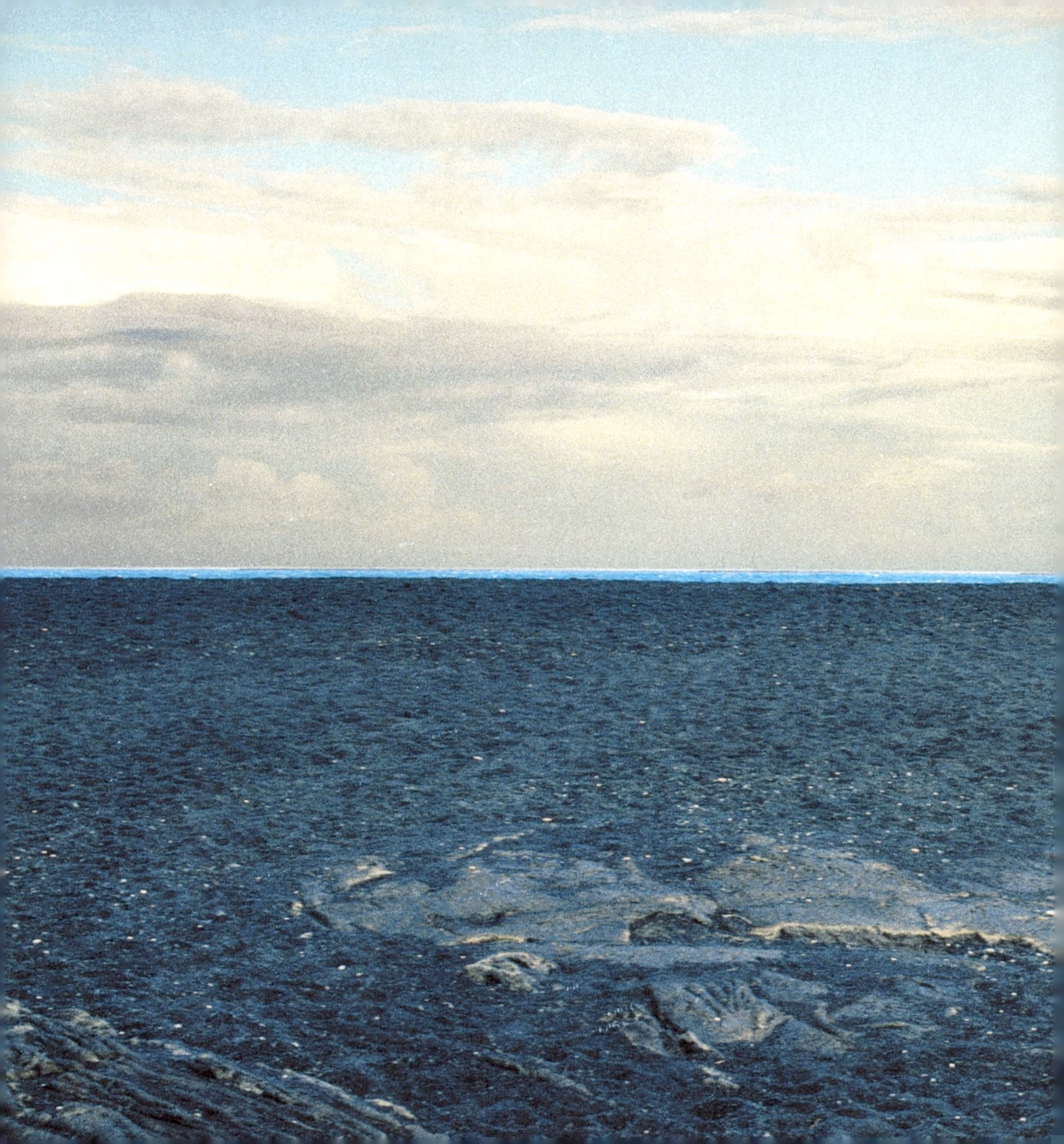

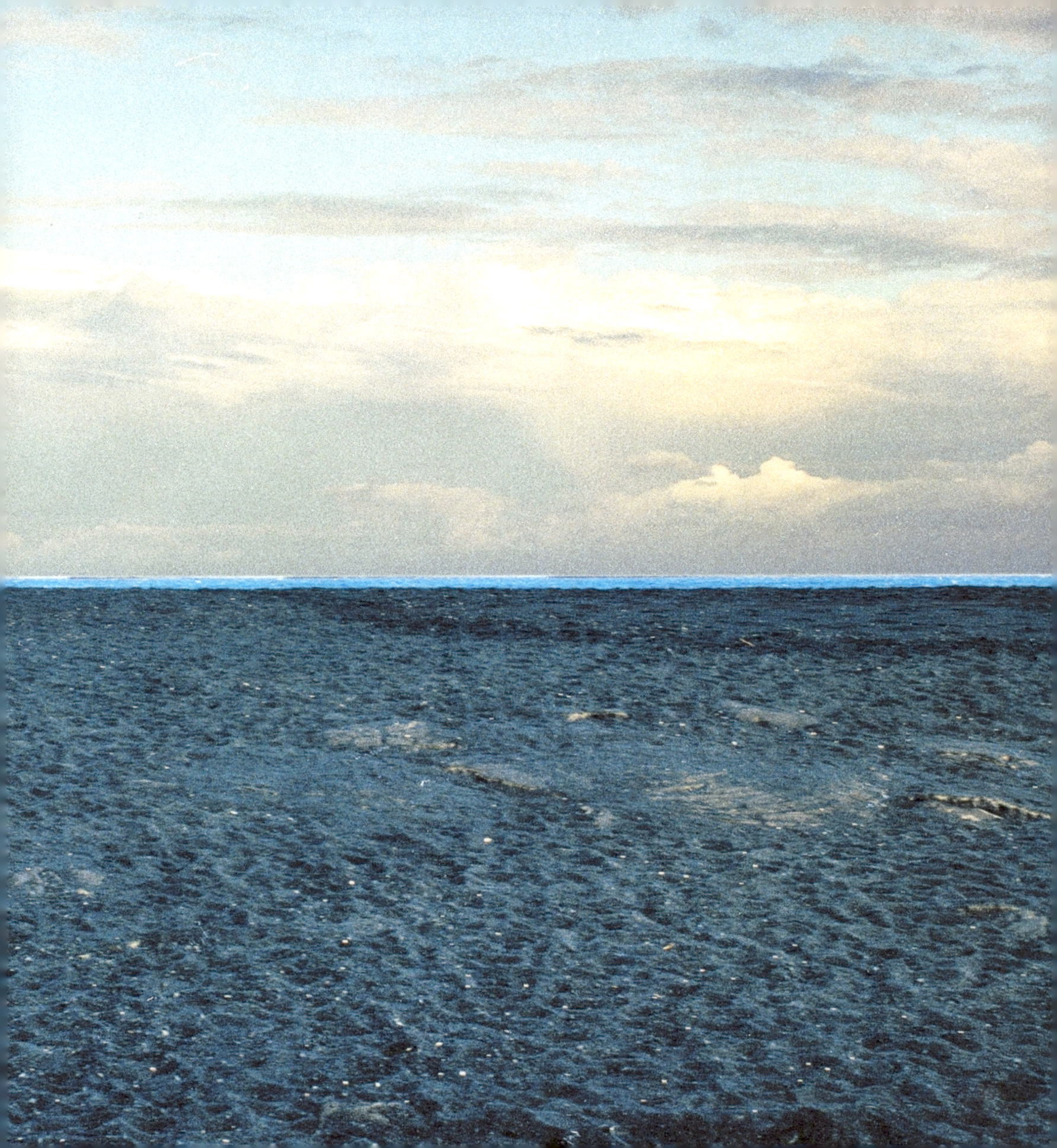

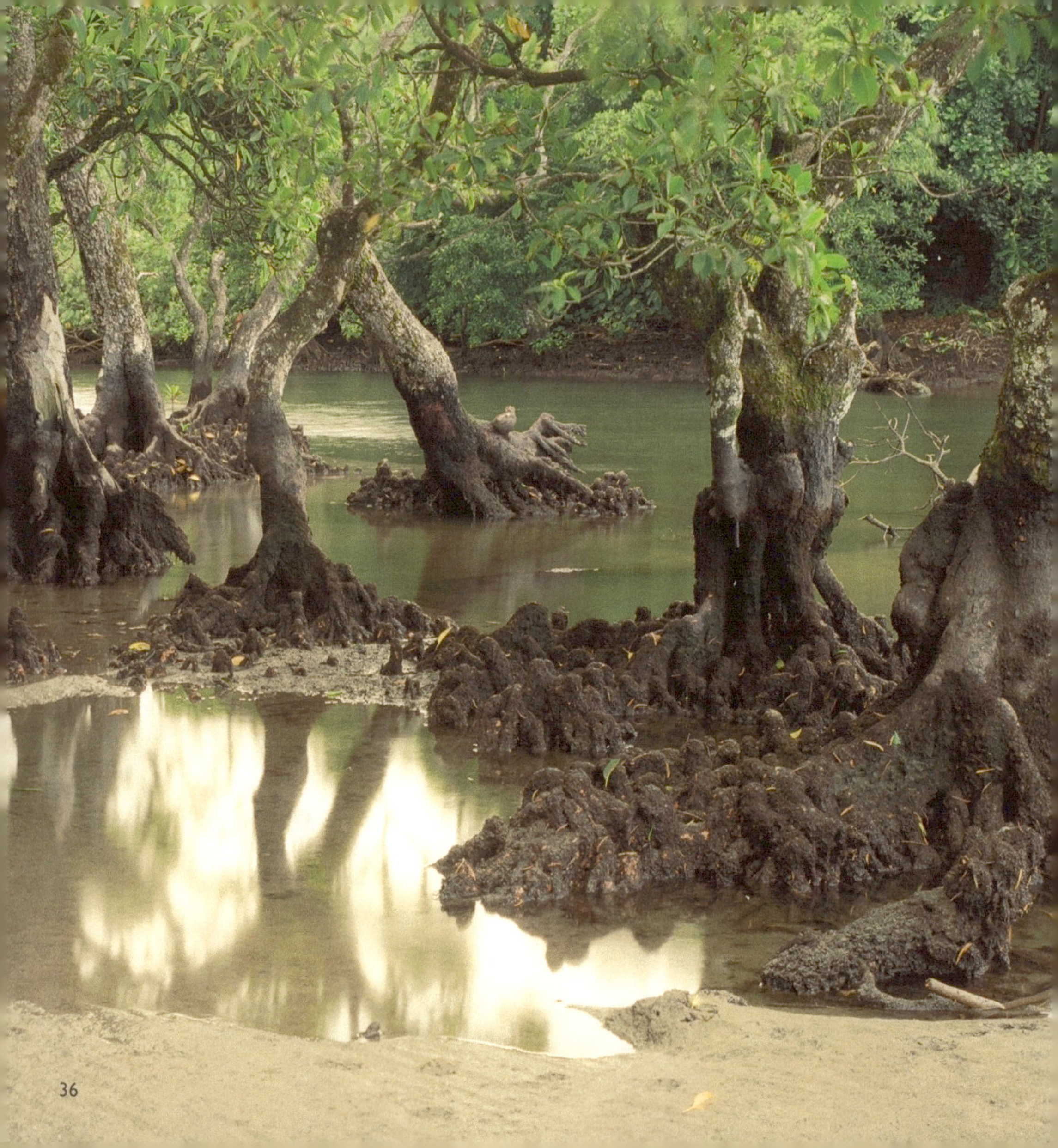

Biota

Over the course of evolution, floating plants and seeds dispersed by the wind, currents, and sea birds colonized Polynesia's distant outposts of land. Many of the arrivals, having gained a foothold on an island, evolved into unique species that are found nowhere else in the world. Threatened by habitat loss and exotic floral introductions, some of the endemic plants are among Earth's most endangered lifeforms. Where they thrive, the native biotas evoke a timeless Polynesian scene. Early one morning, catching the incoming tide, I paddled my outrigger canoe into a protected estuary on Upolu Island in Samoa and floated in its crystal-clear water amid the gnarly buttress roots of mangroves. Native plants surrounded me, and I imagined myself being among the first persons to have entered that pristine habitat.

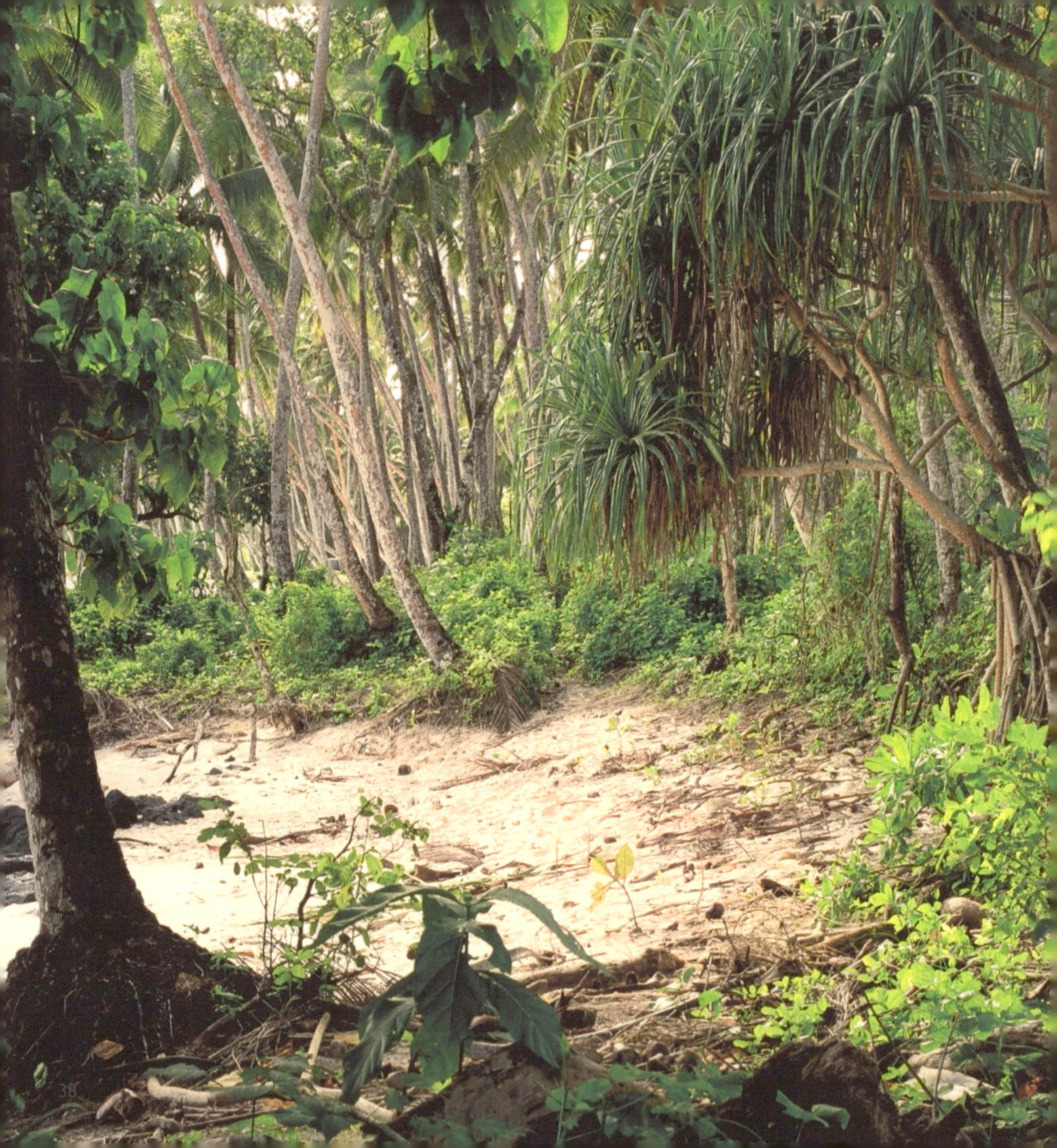

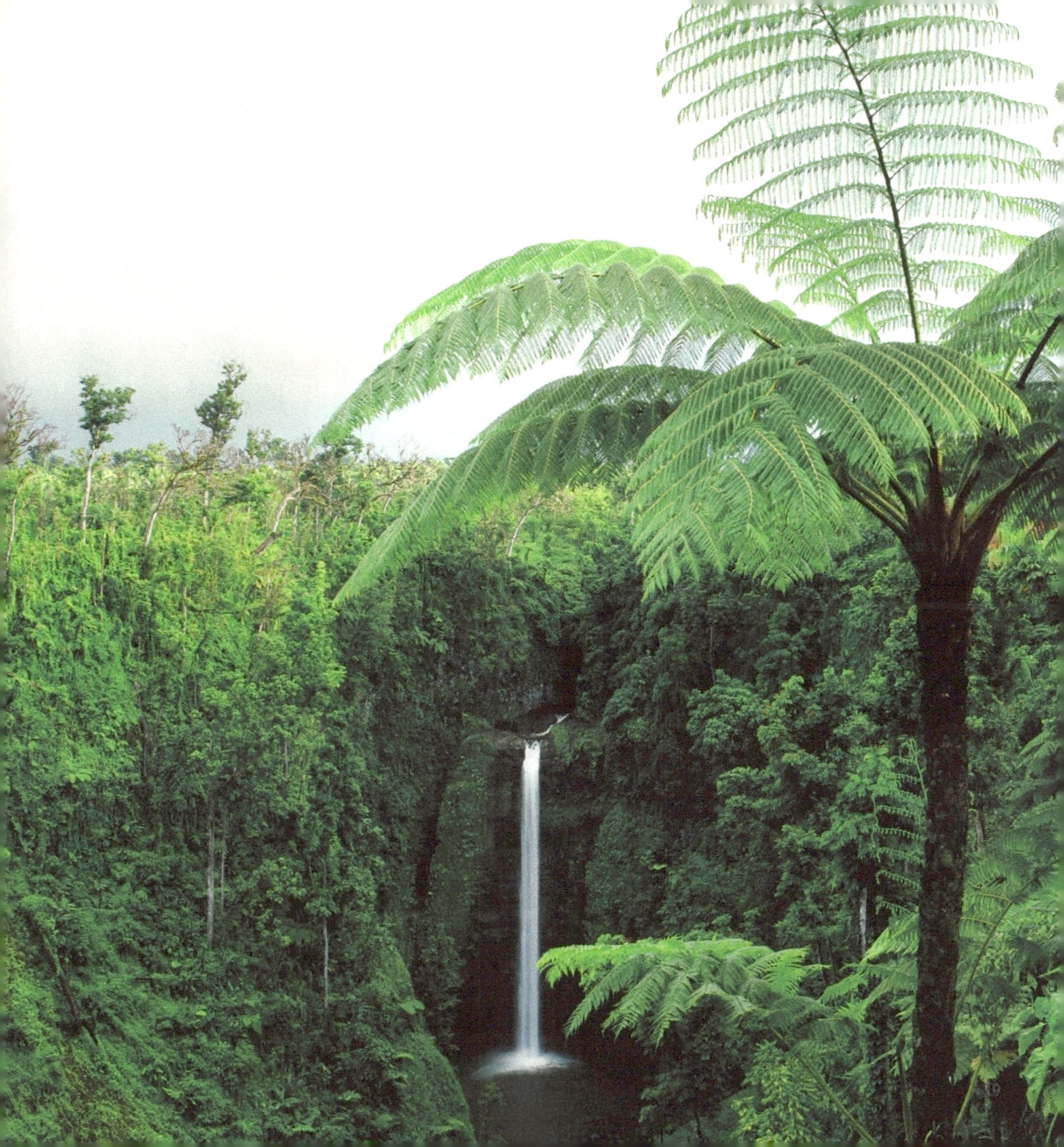

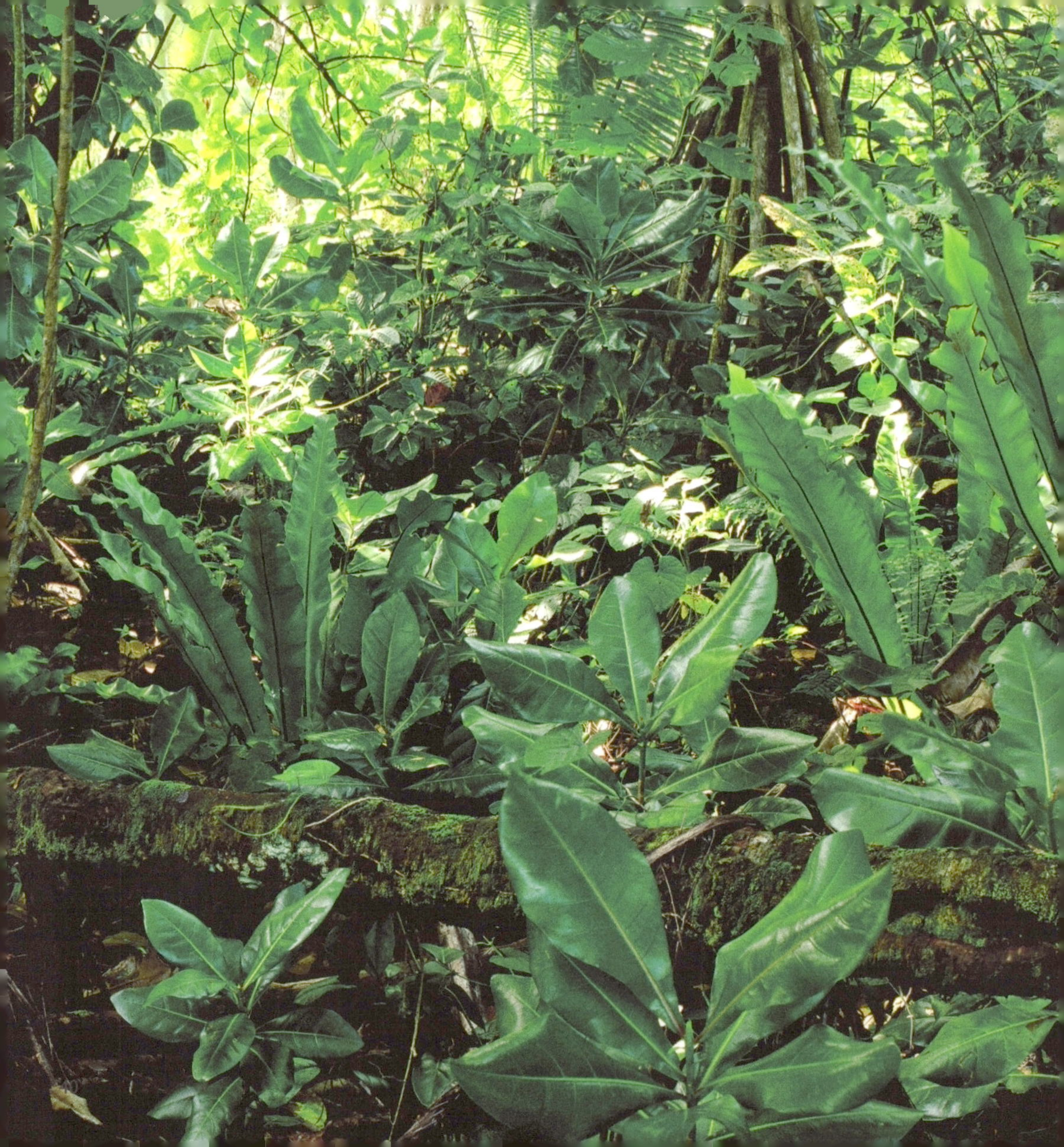

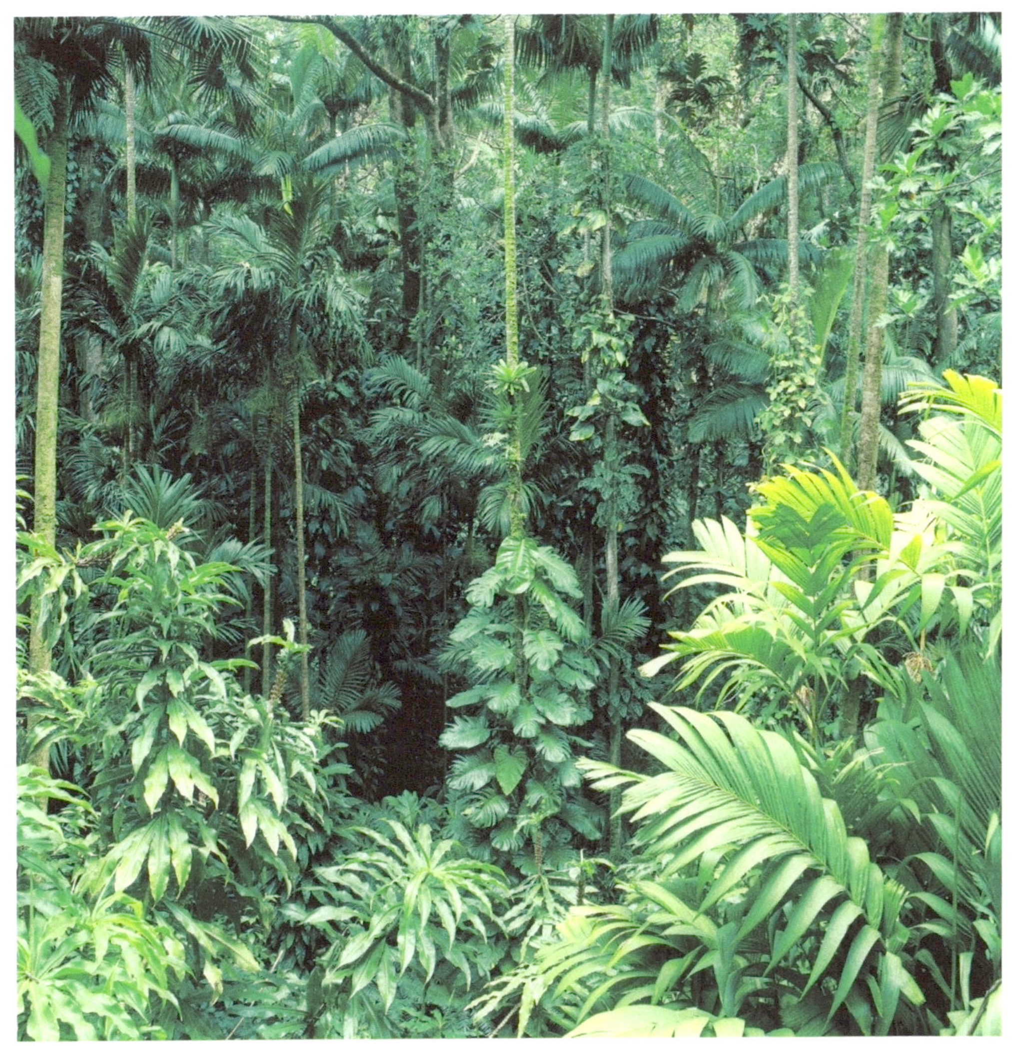

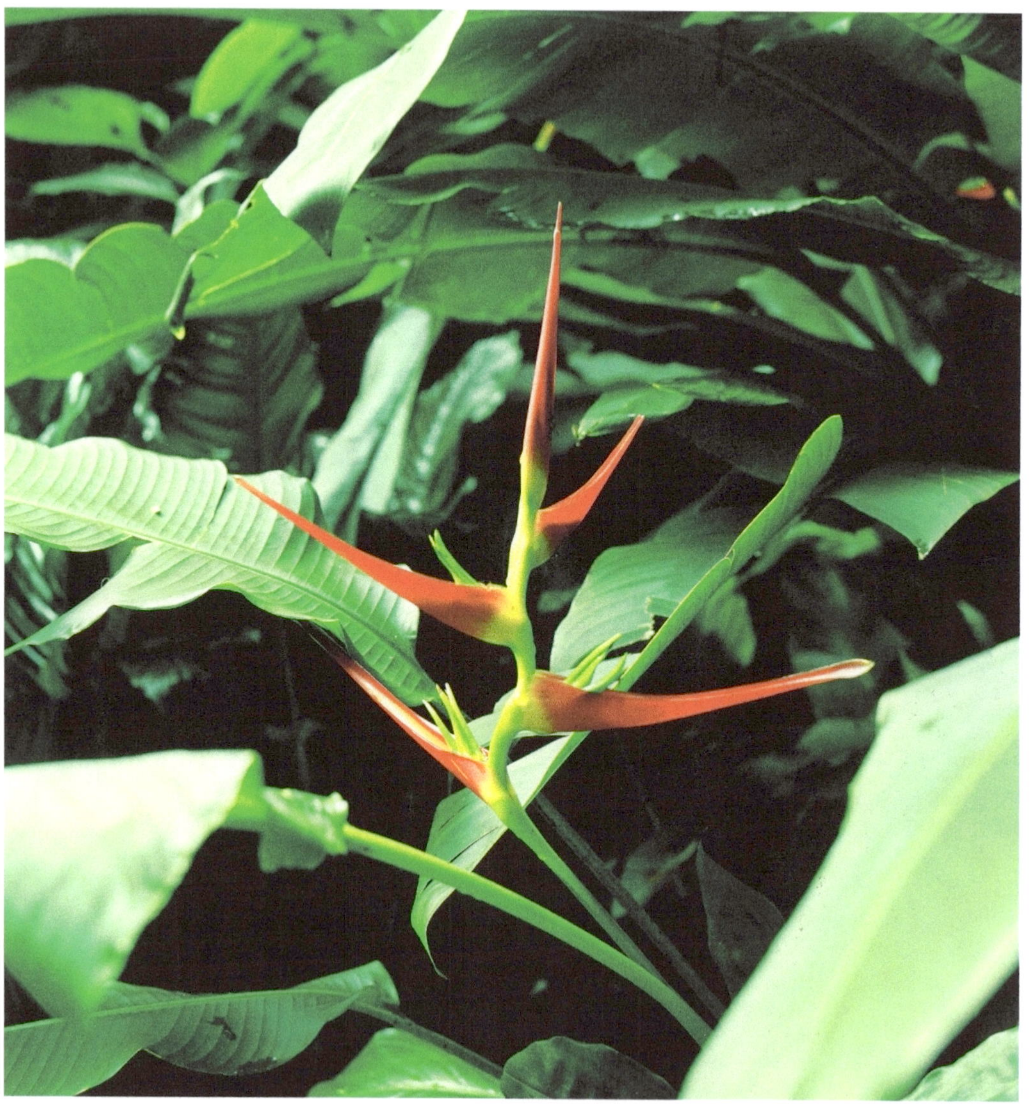

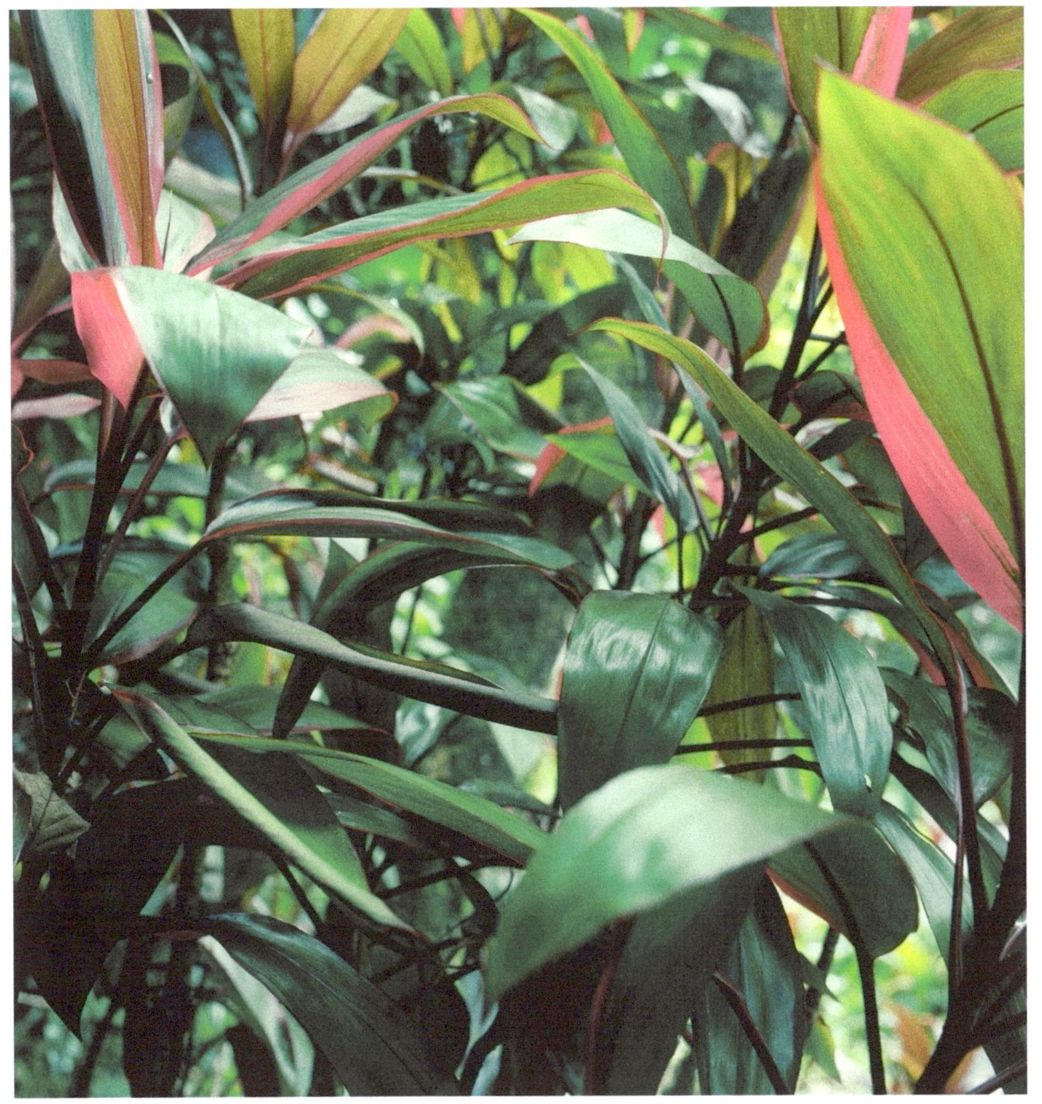

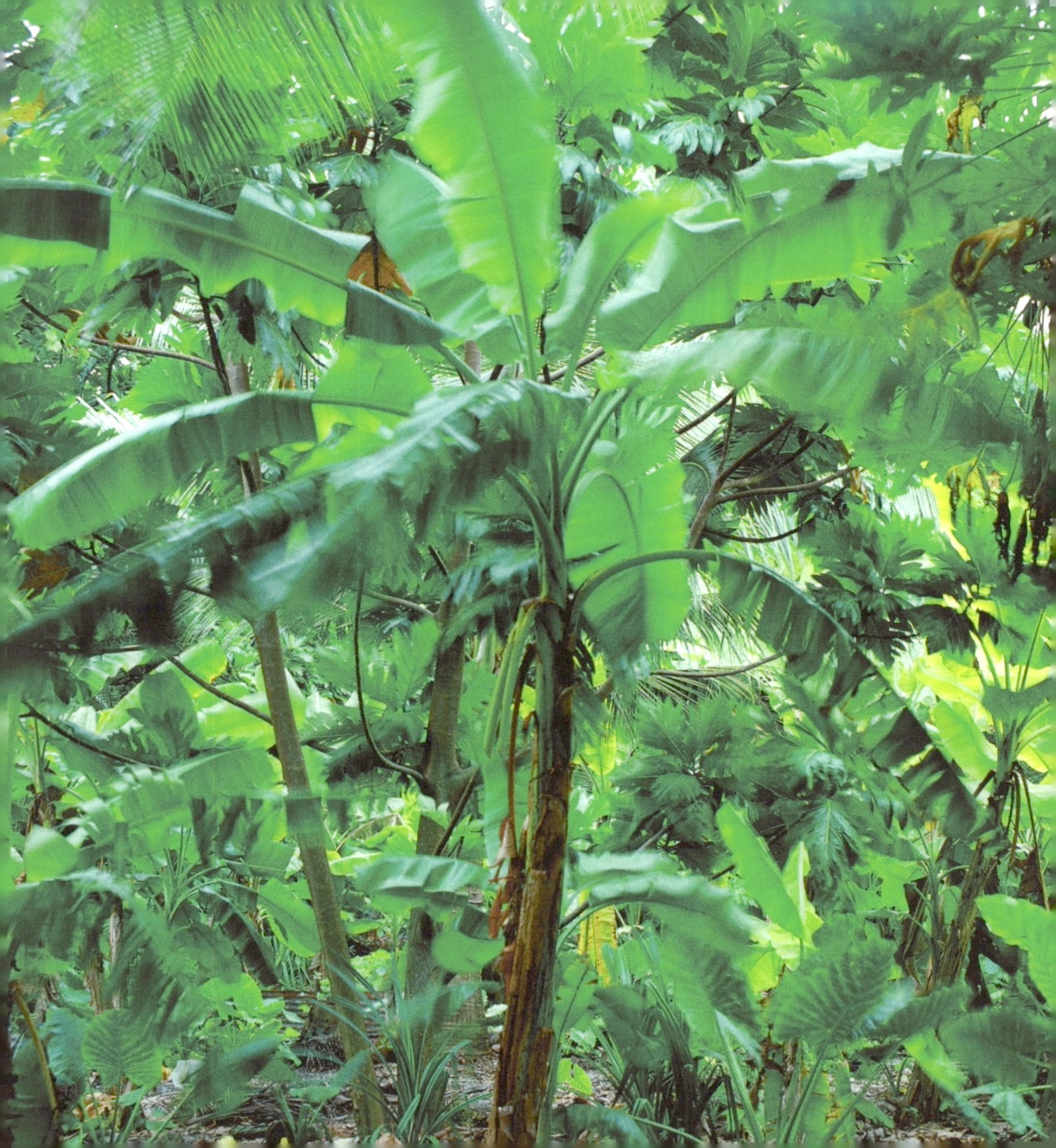

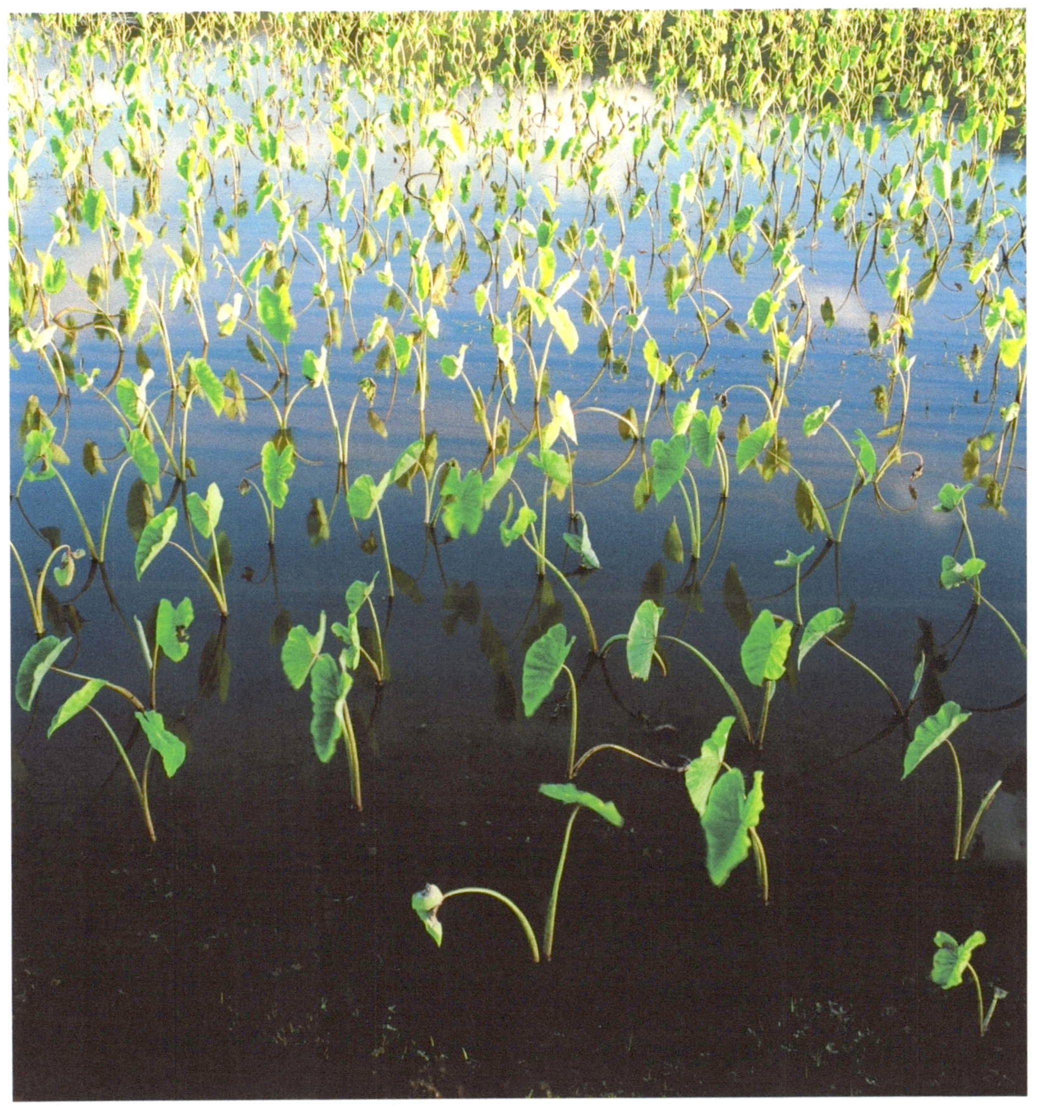

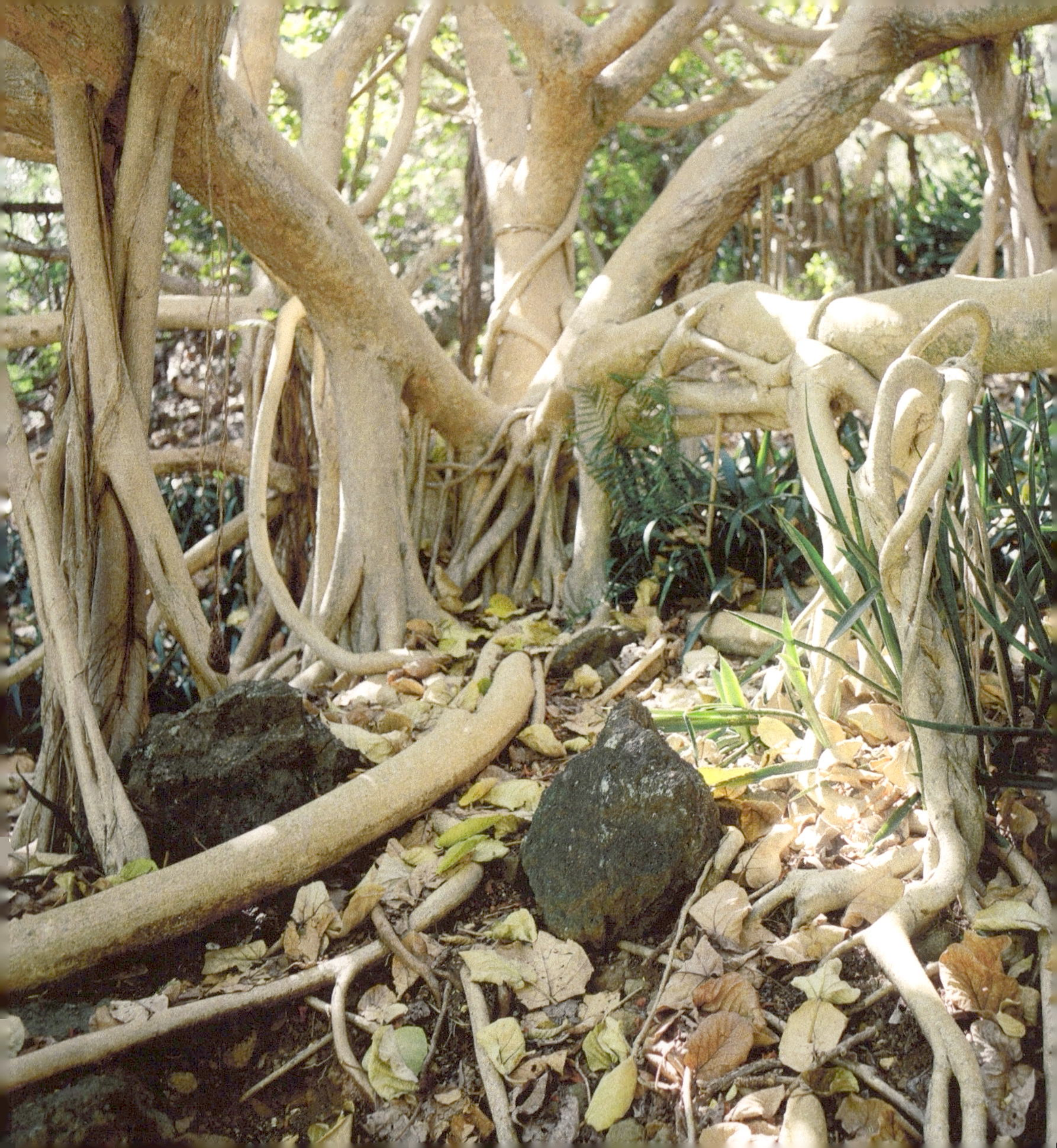

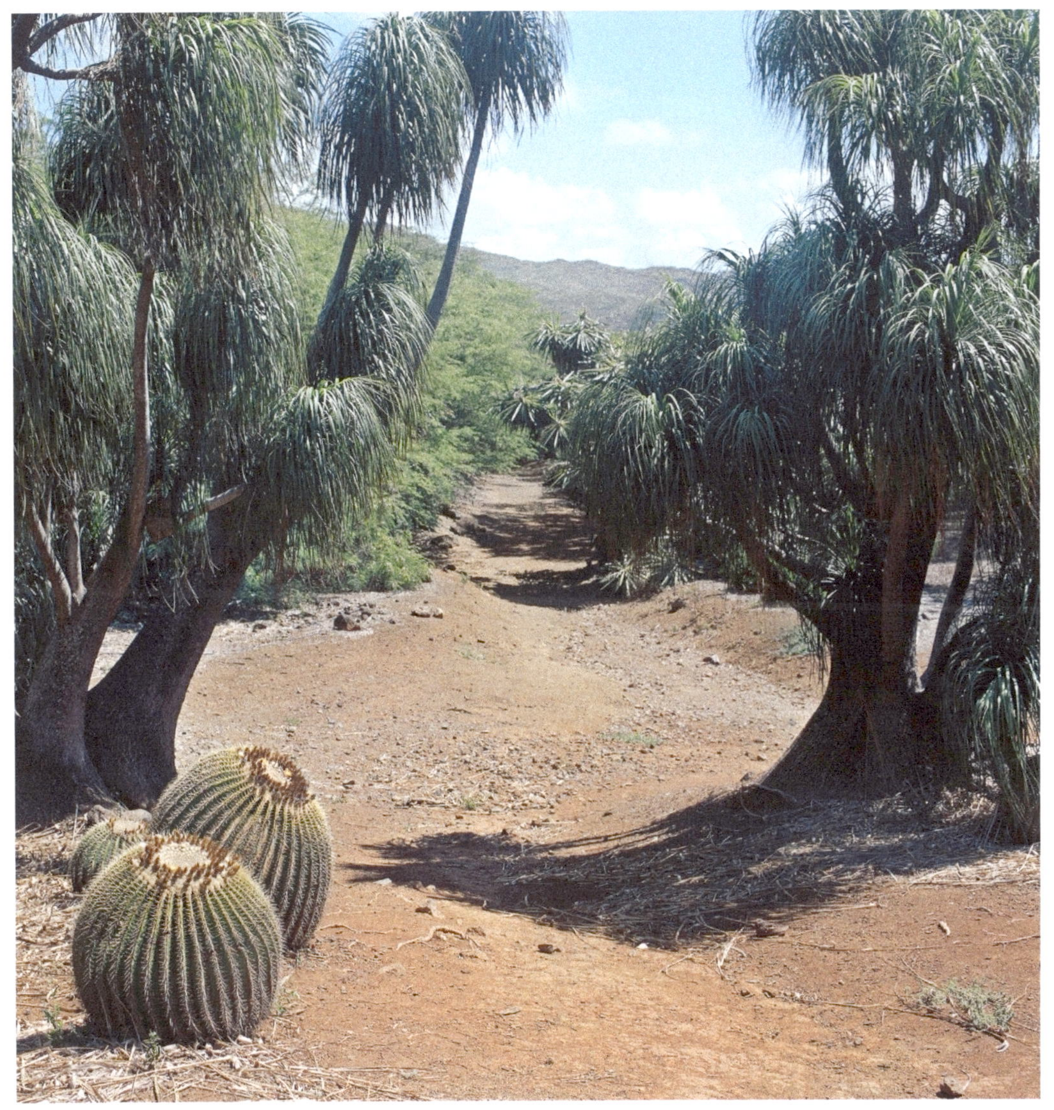

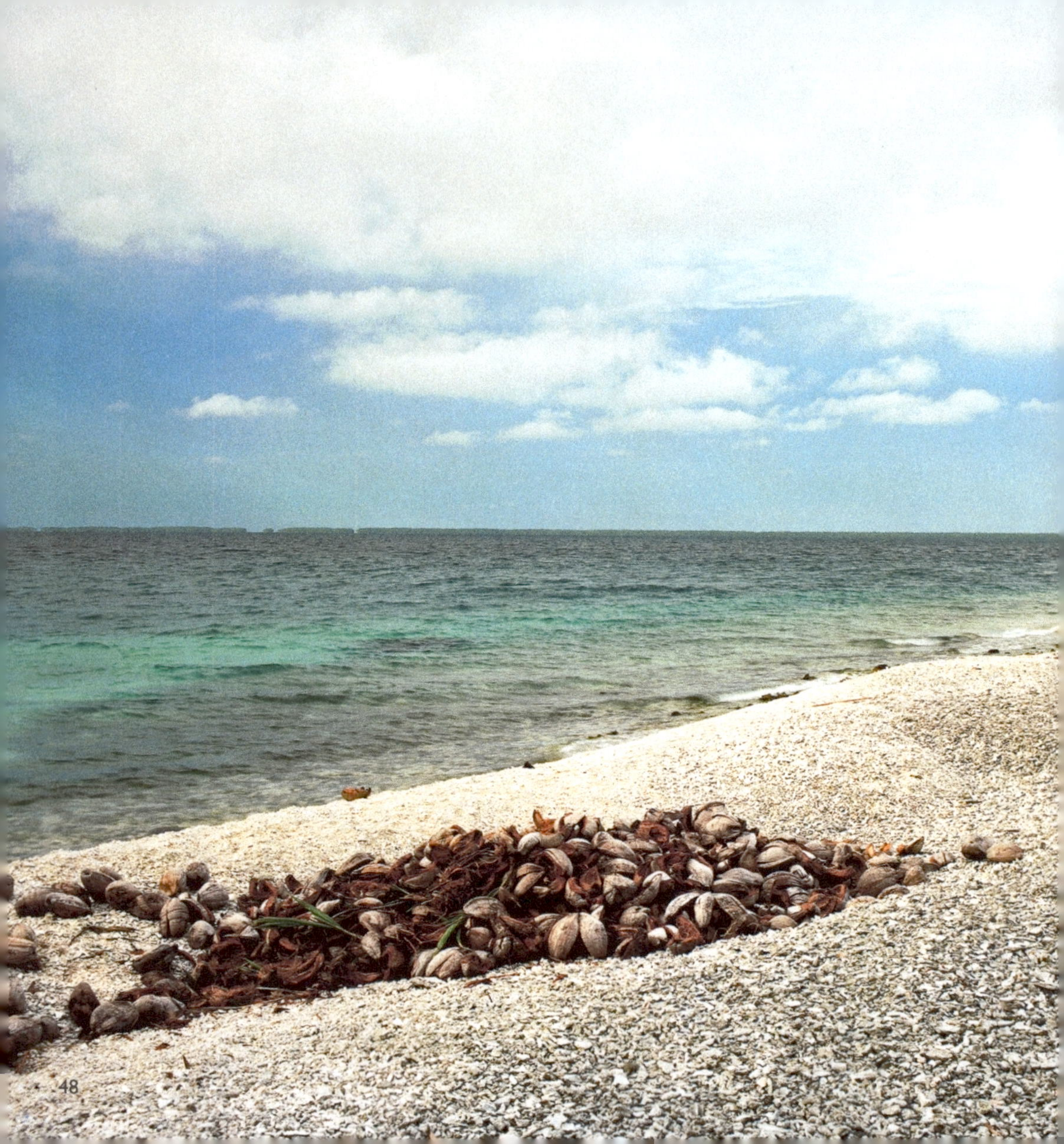

Three bold coconuts crossed
oceans of universe searching
a place to be born.

— Kauraka Kauraka (1951–1997)
Cook Island poet

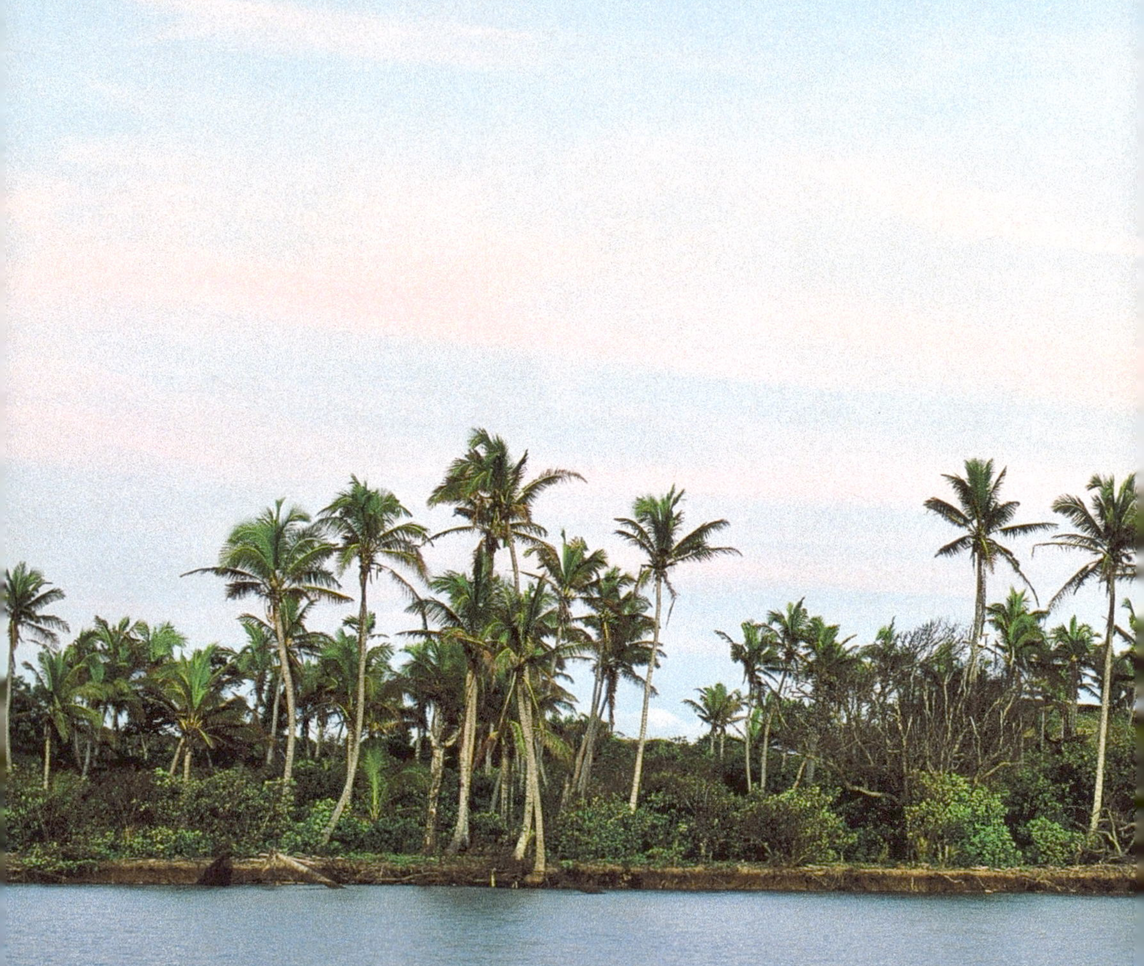

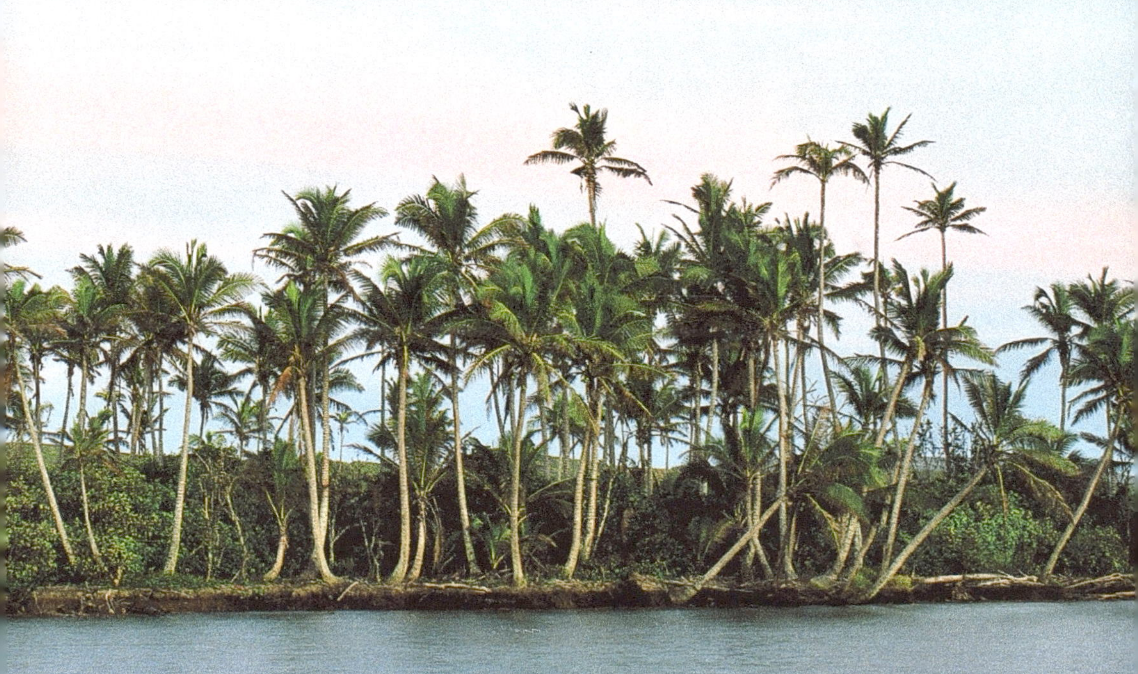

Seafarers

Mariners from Southeast Asia sailed in fleets of voyaging canoes across the Pacific Ocean more than three thousand years ago, using star navigation and their knowledge of the sea and sky to find their way. They settled on the inhabitable islands, developed into a unique culture, and became the Polynesians. Tangible evidence of this remarkable history is in the Sigatoka dunes on Viti Levu island where I came across shards of Lapita pottery poking out from the sand. Archaeologists use these ceramic tracings, which are found throughout Polynesia, to puzzle out the routes of the early voyages. Their presence in the Sigatoka sand indicated that I was standing near an important disembarkation point for the earliest Polynesian sailors.

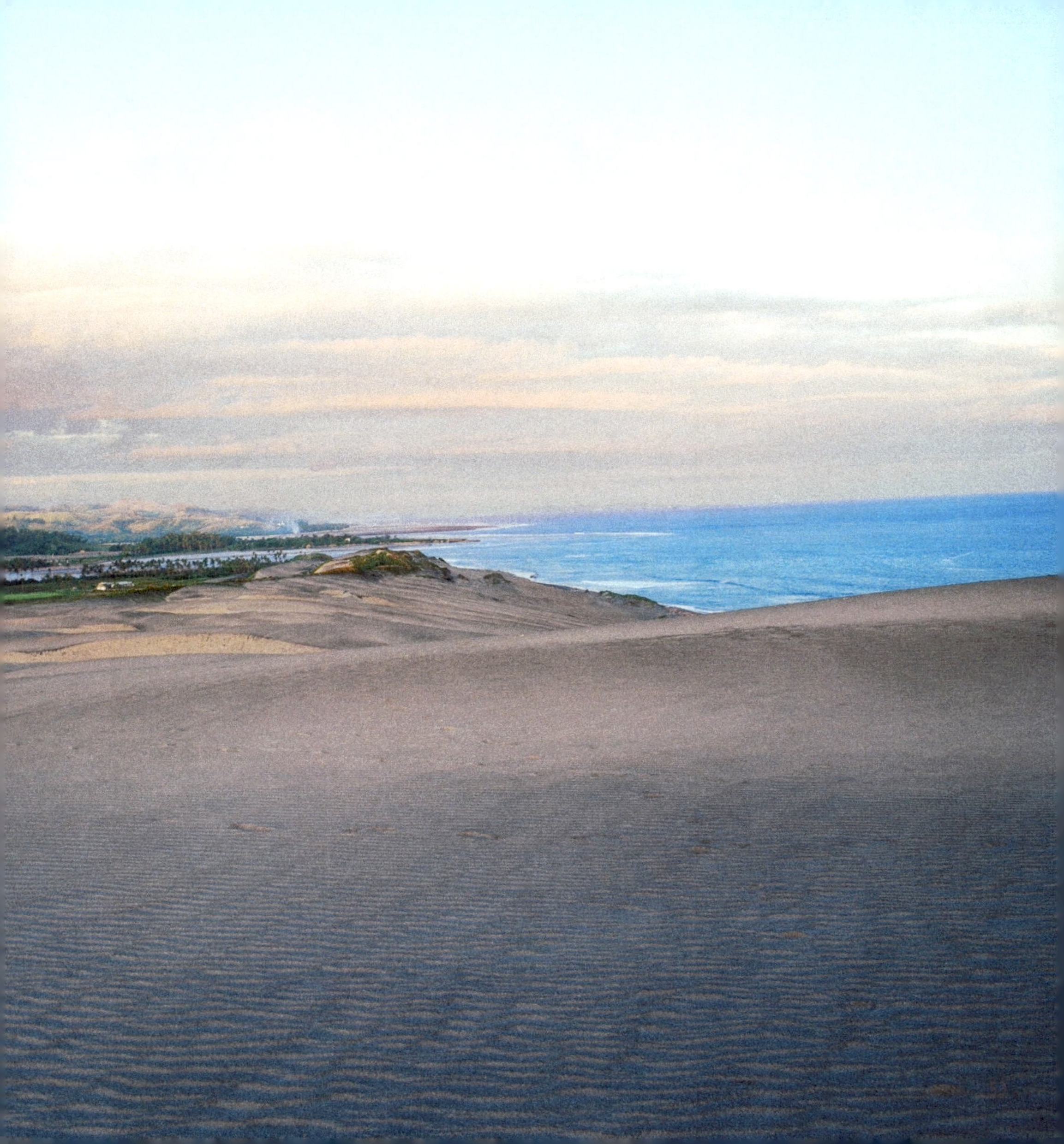

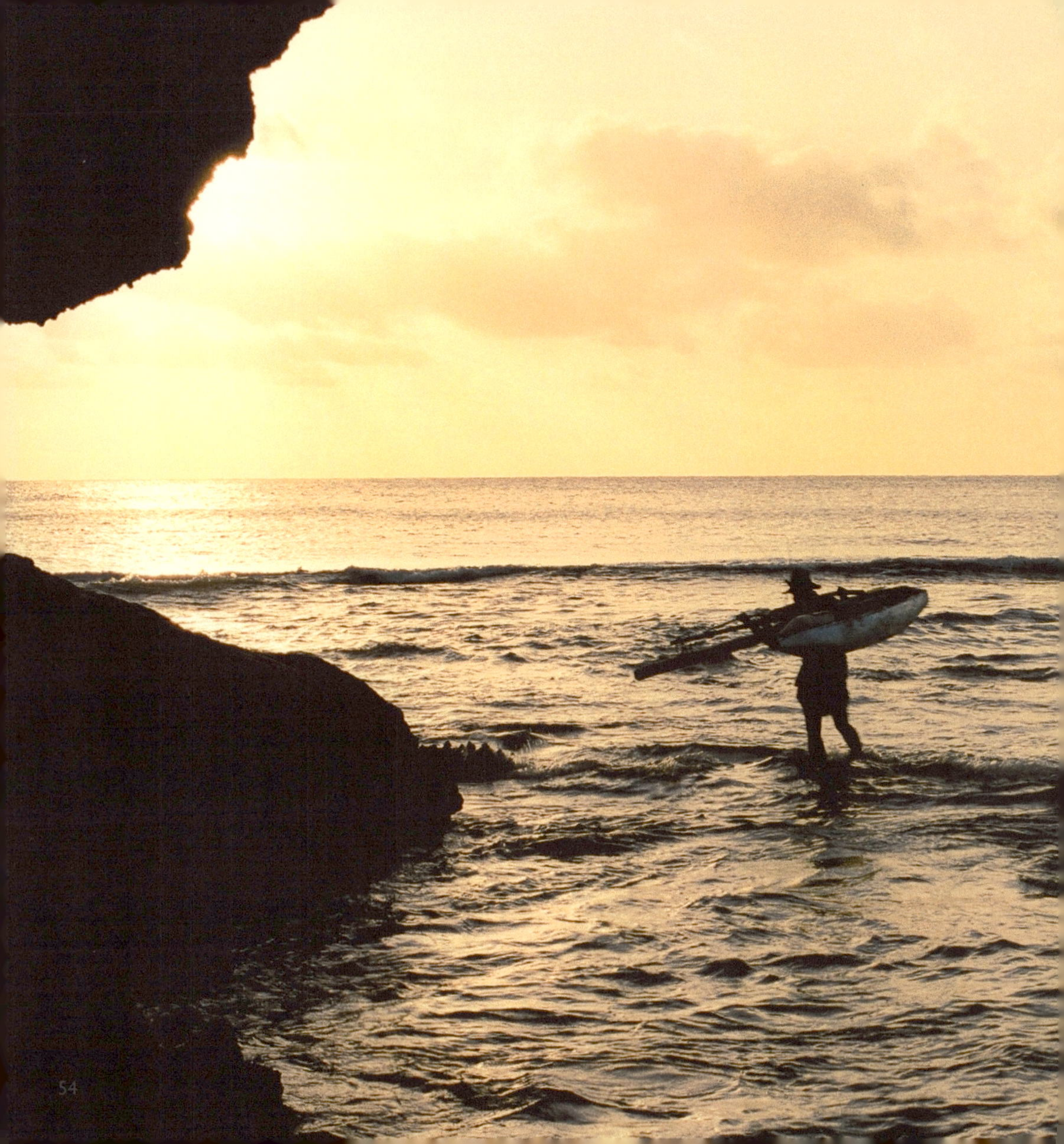

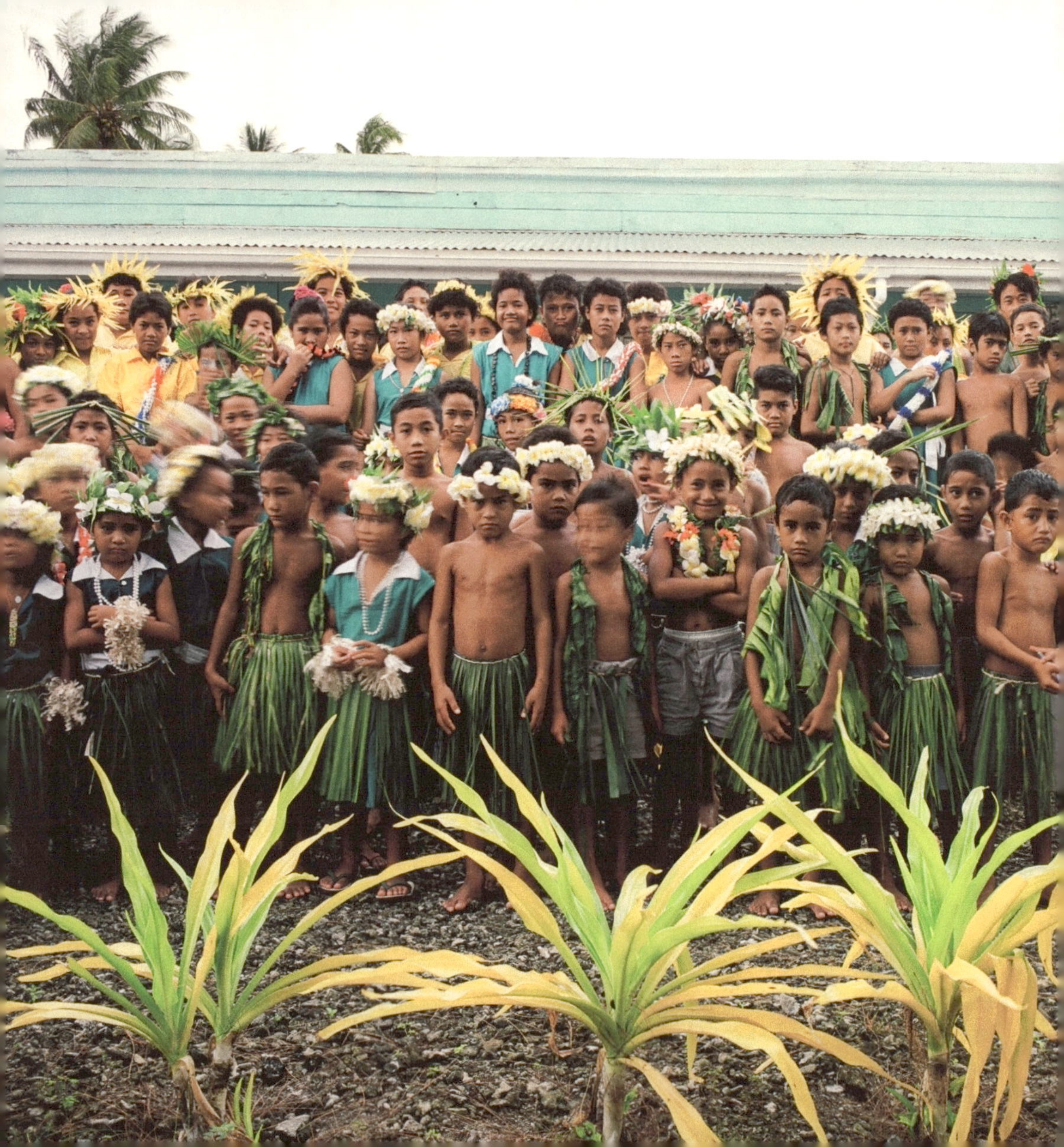

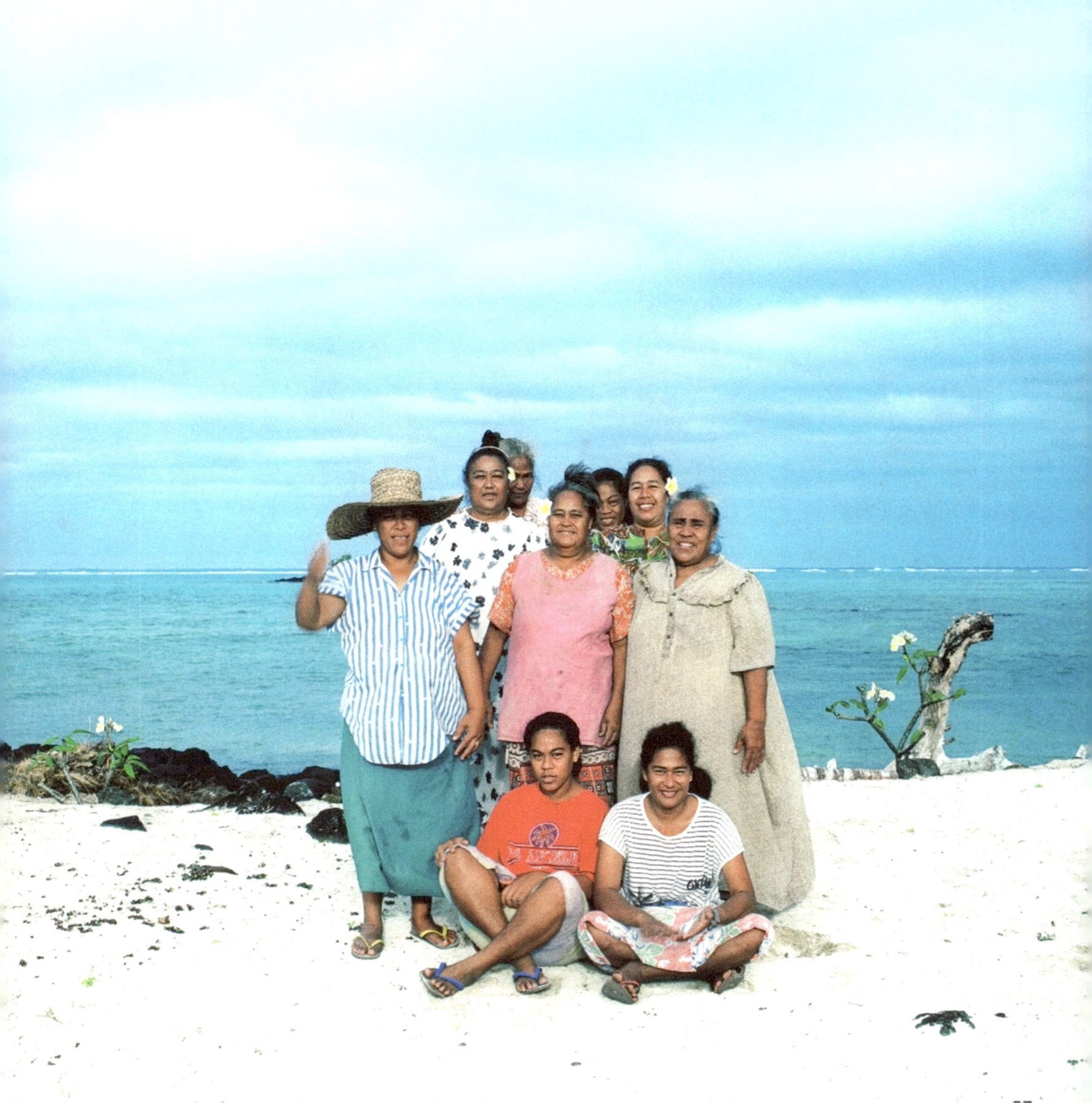

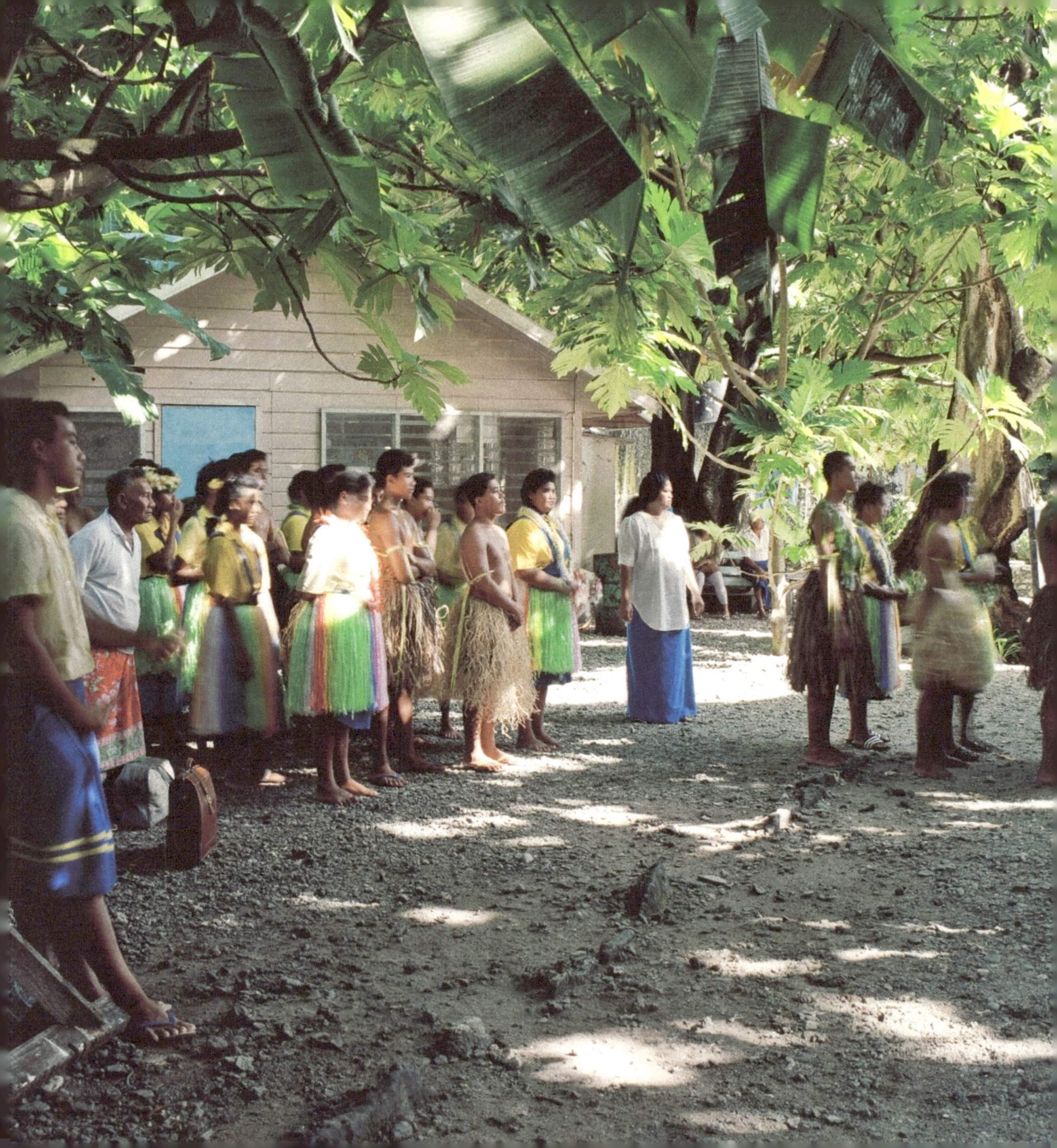

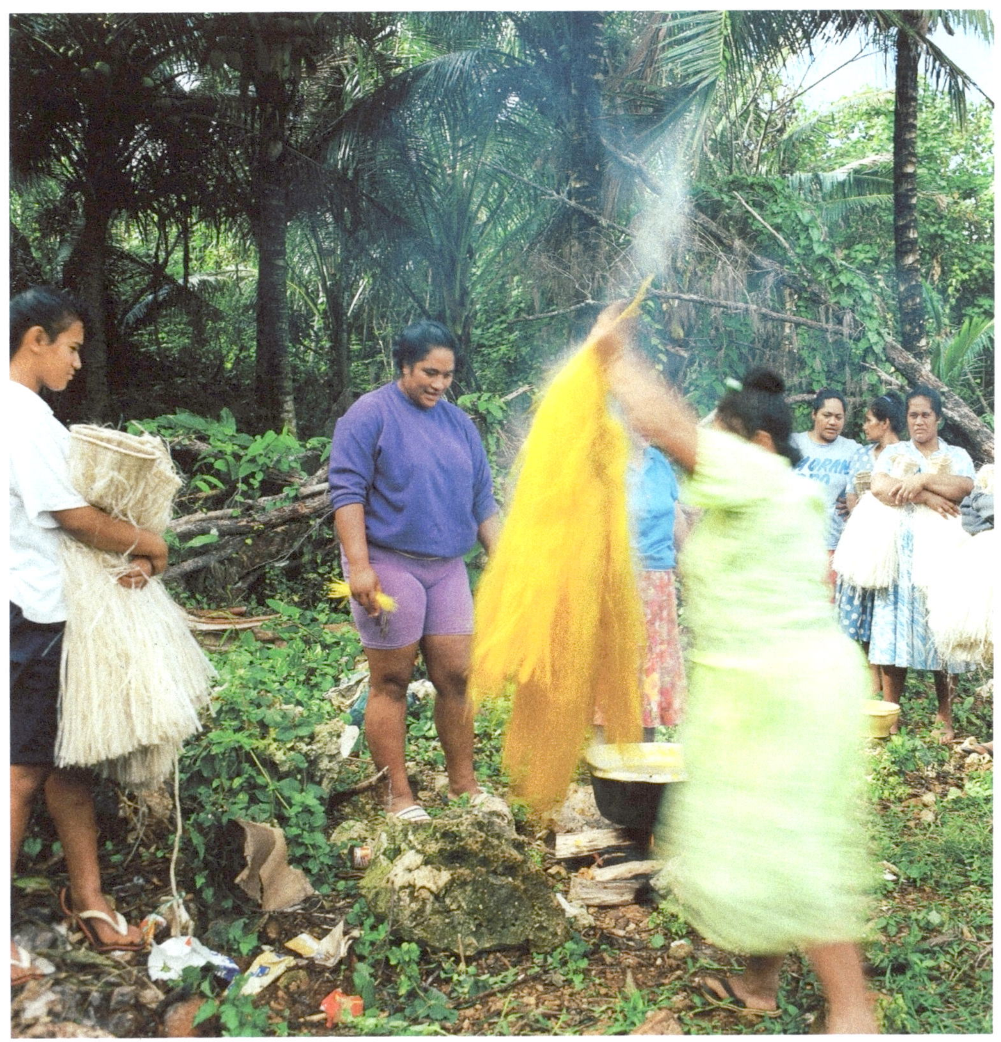

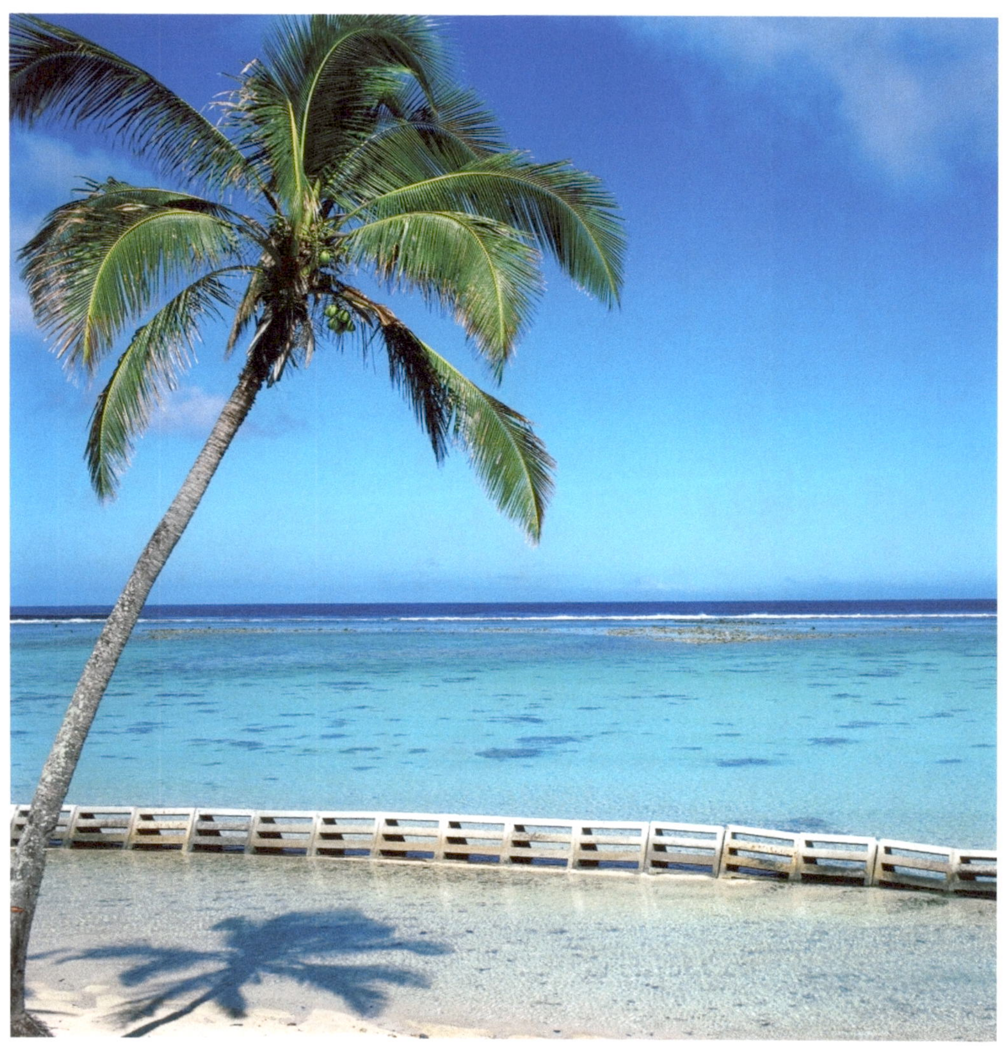

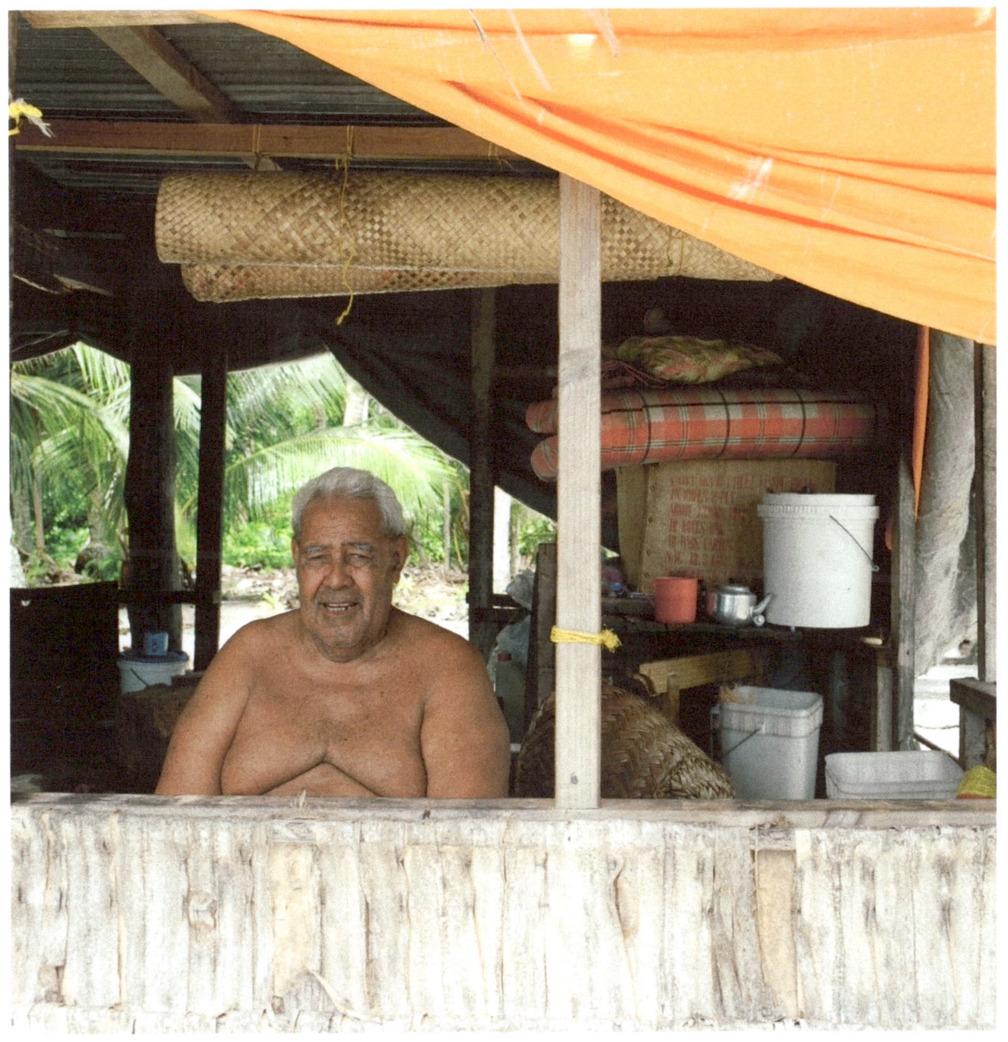

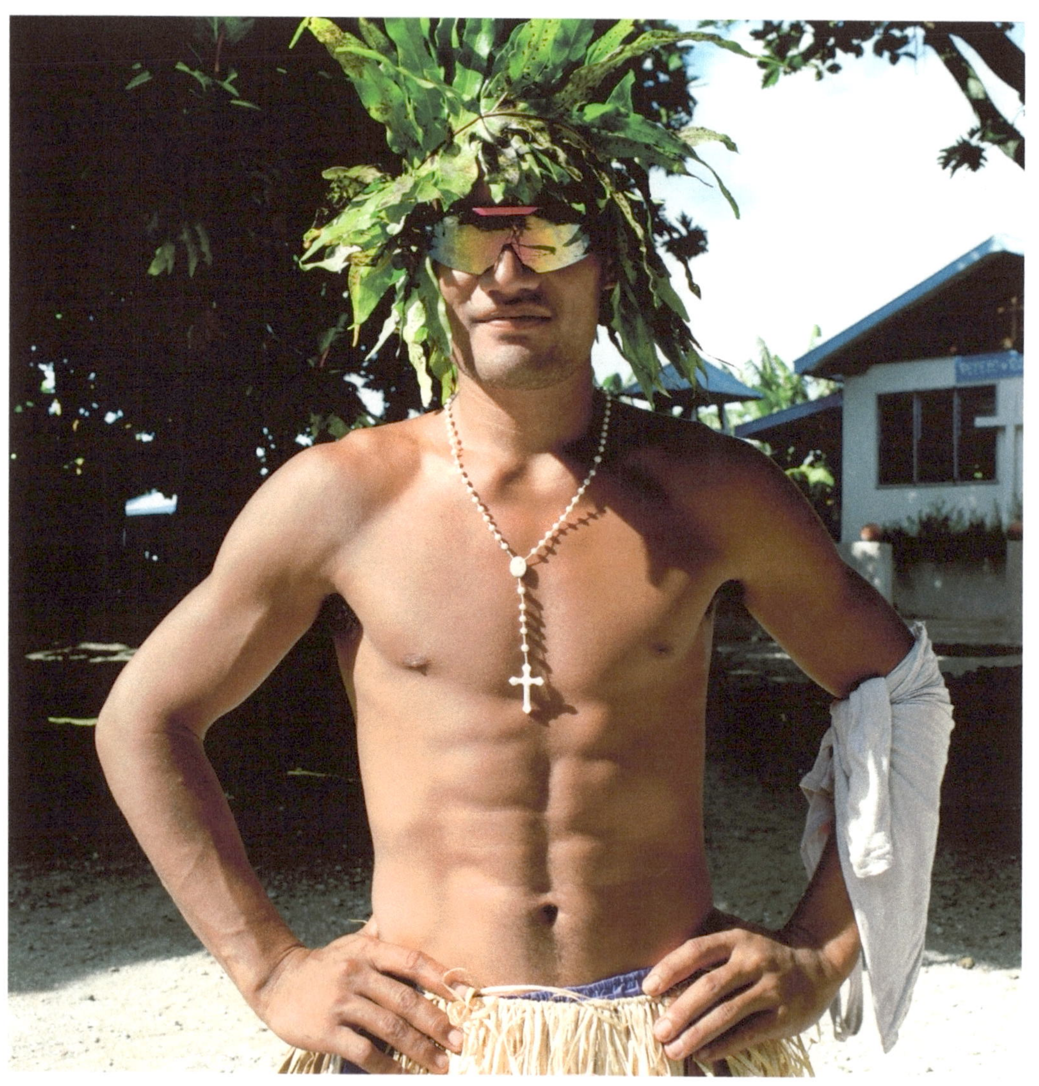

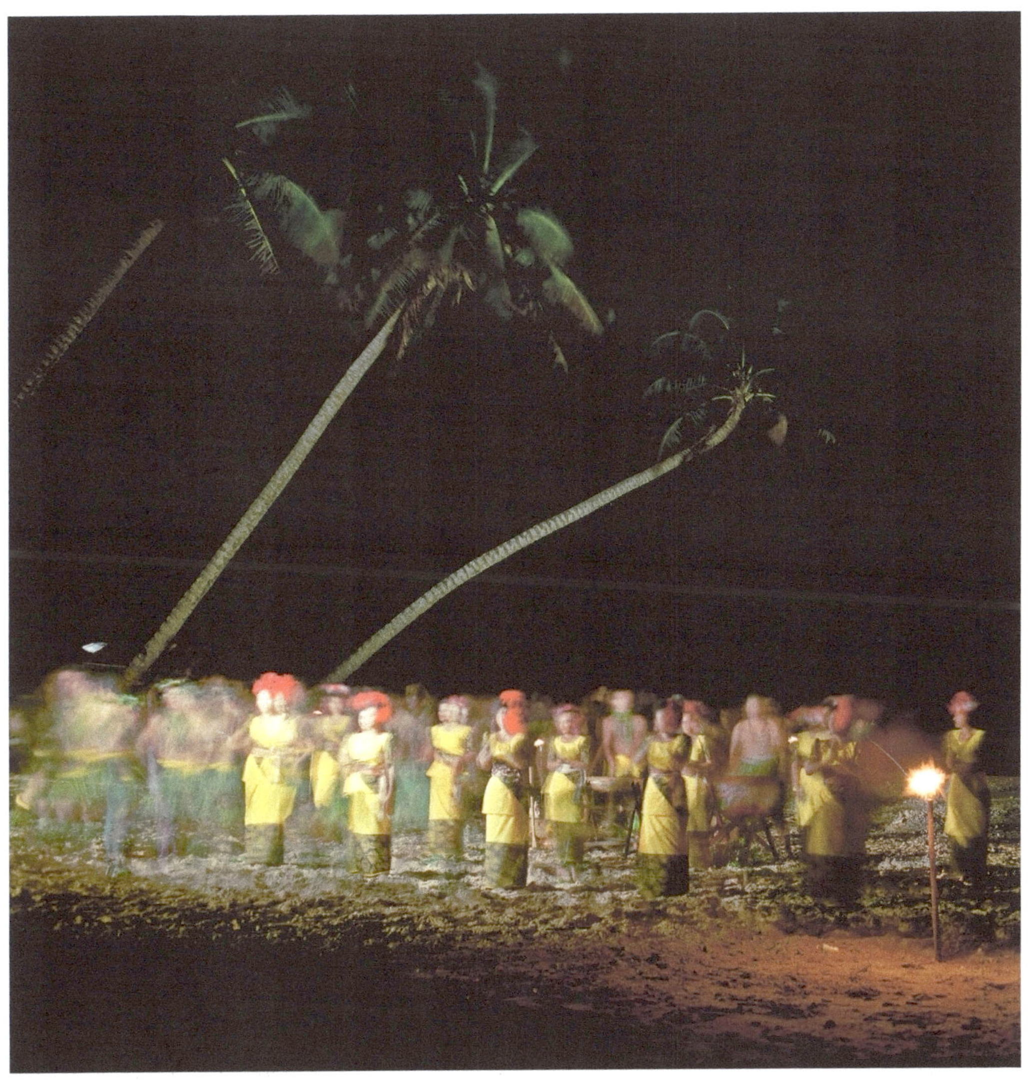

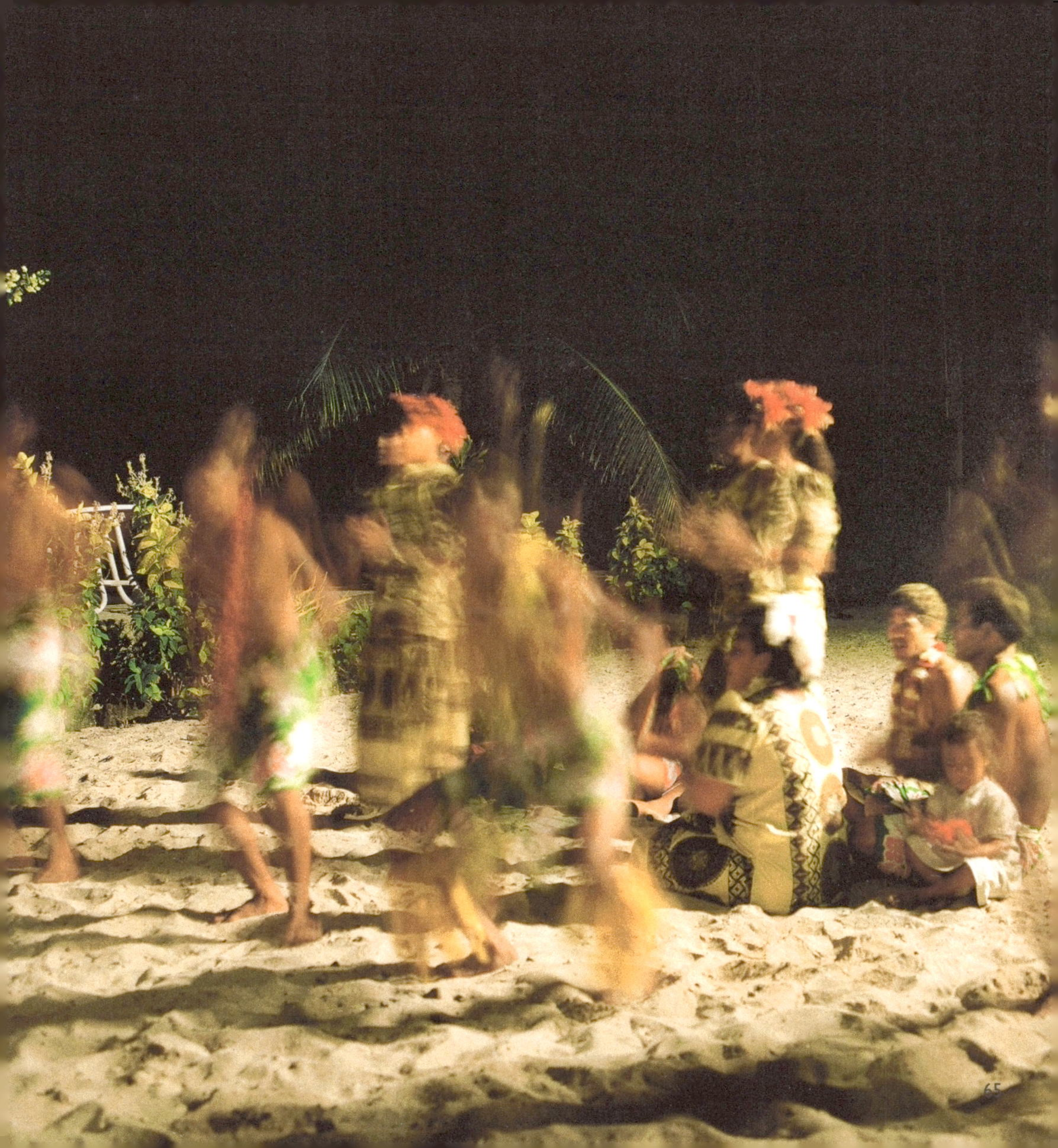

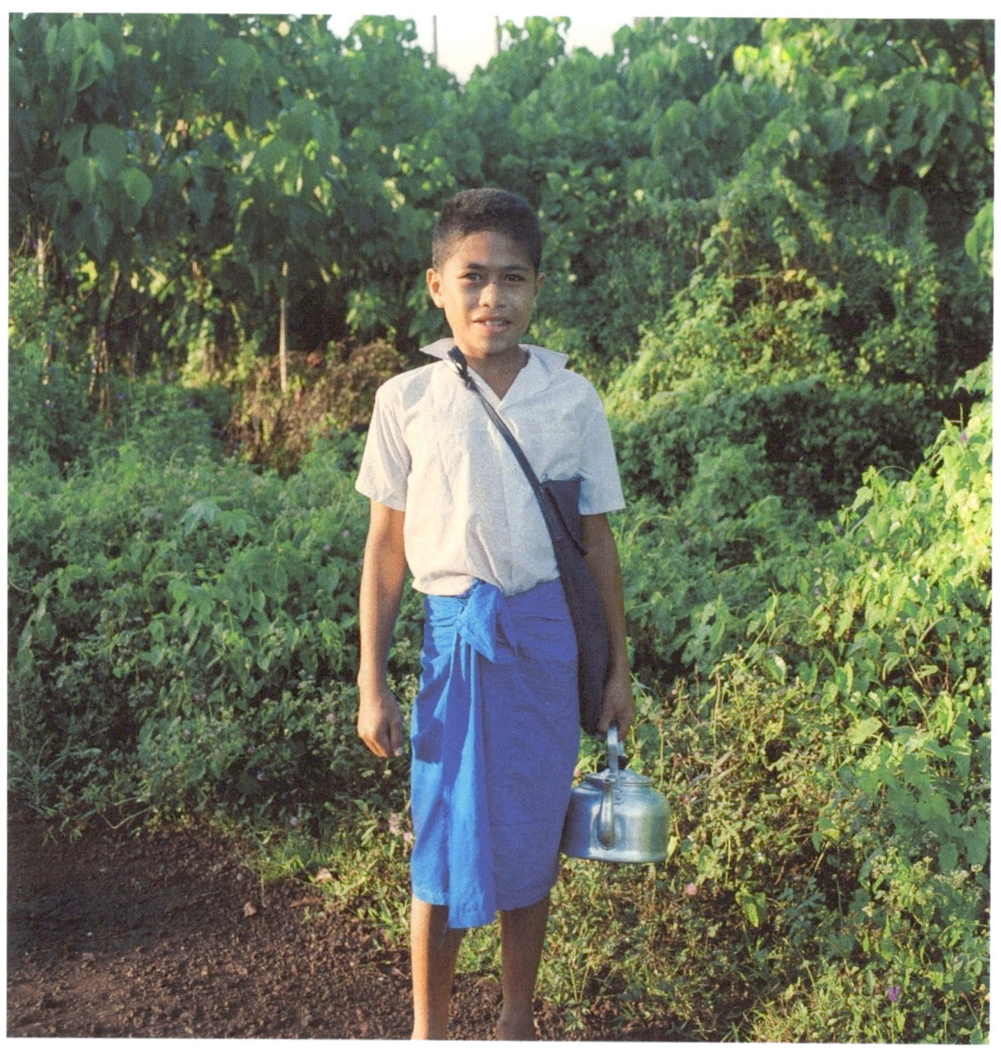

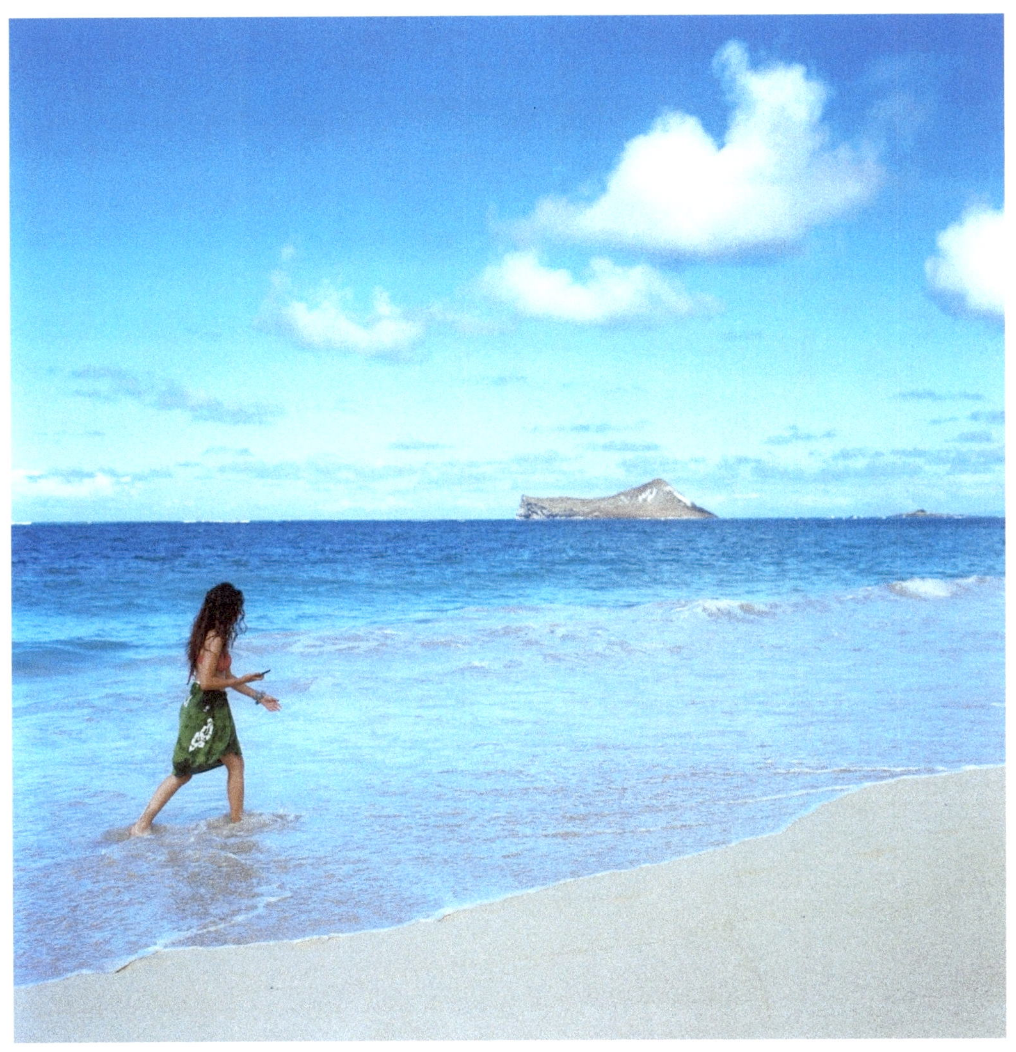

We are the sea, we are the ocean.
Oceania is us.

—'Epeli Hau'ofa (1939–2009),
Tongan writer and anthropologist

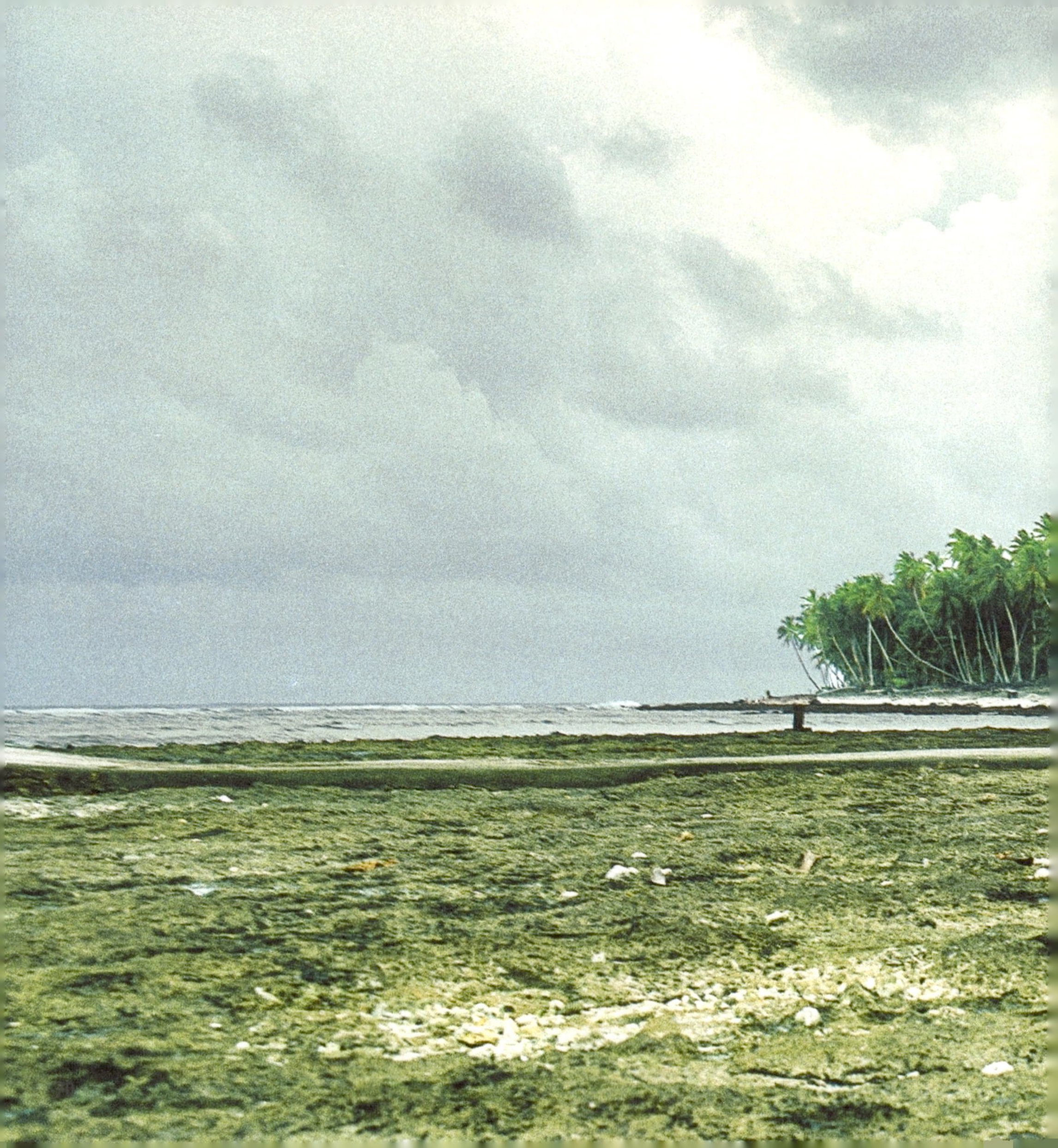

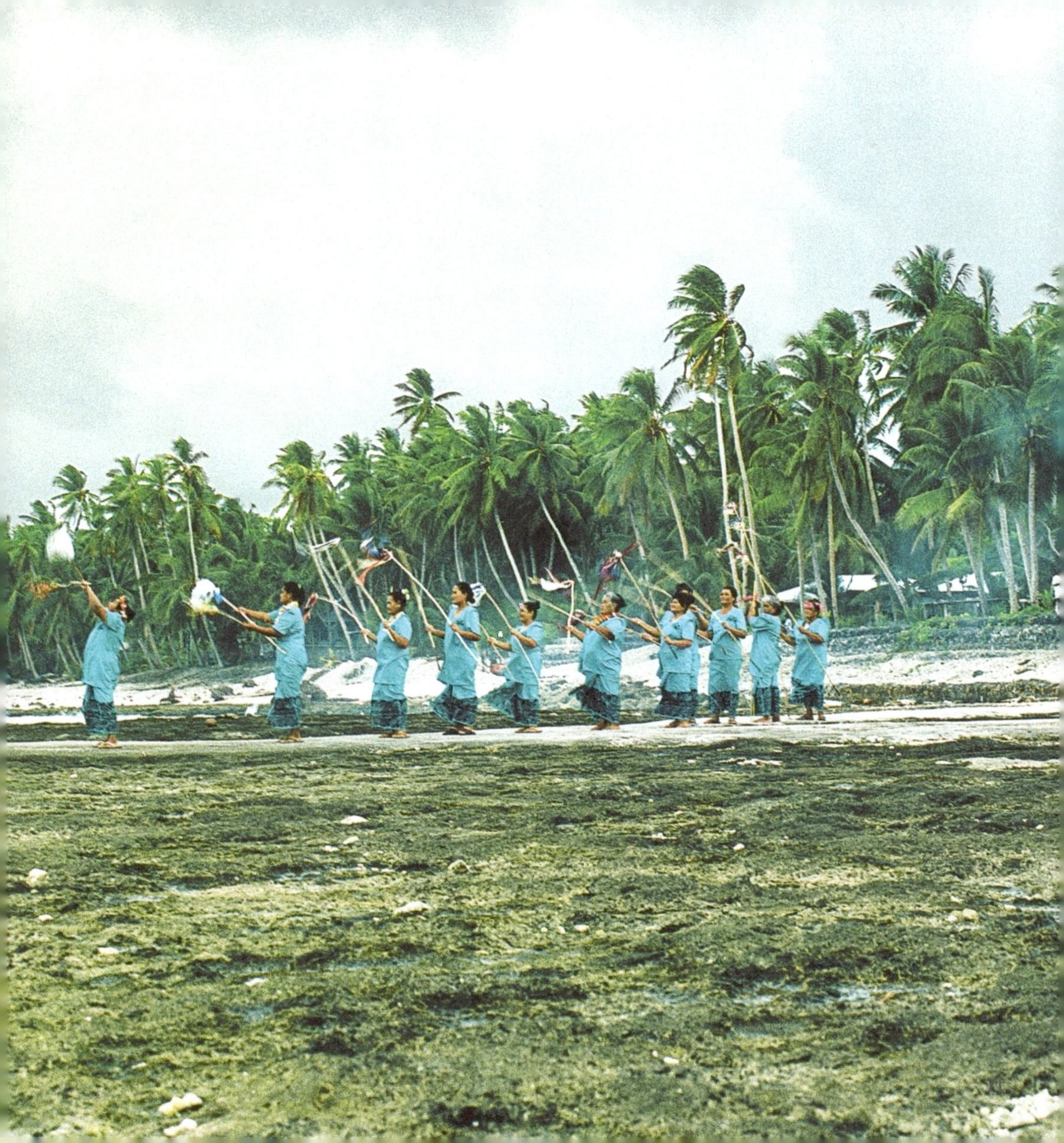

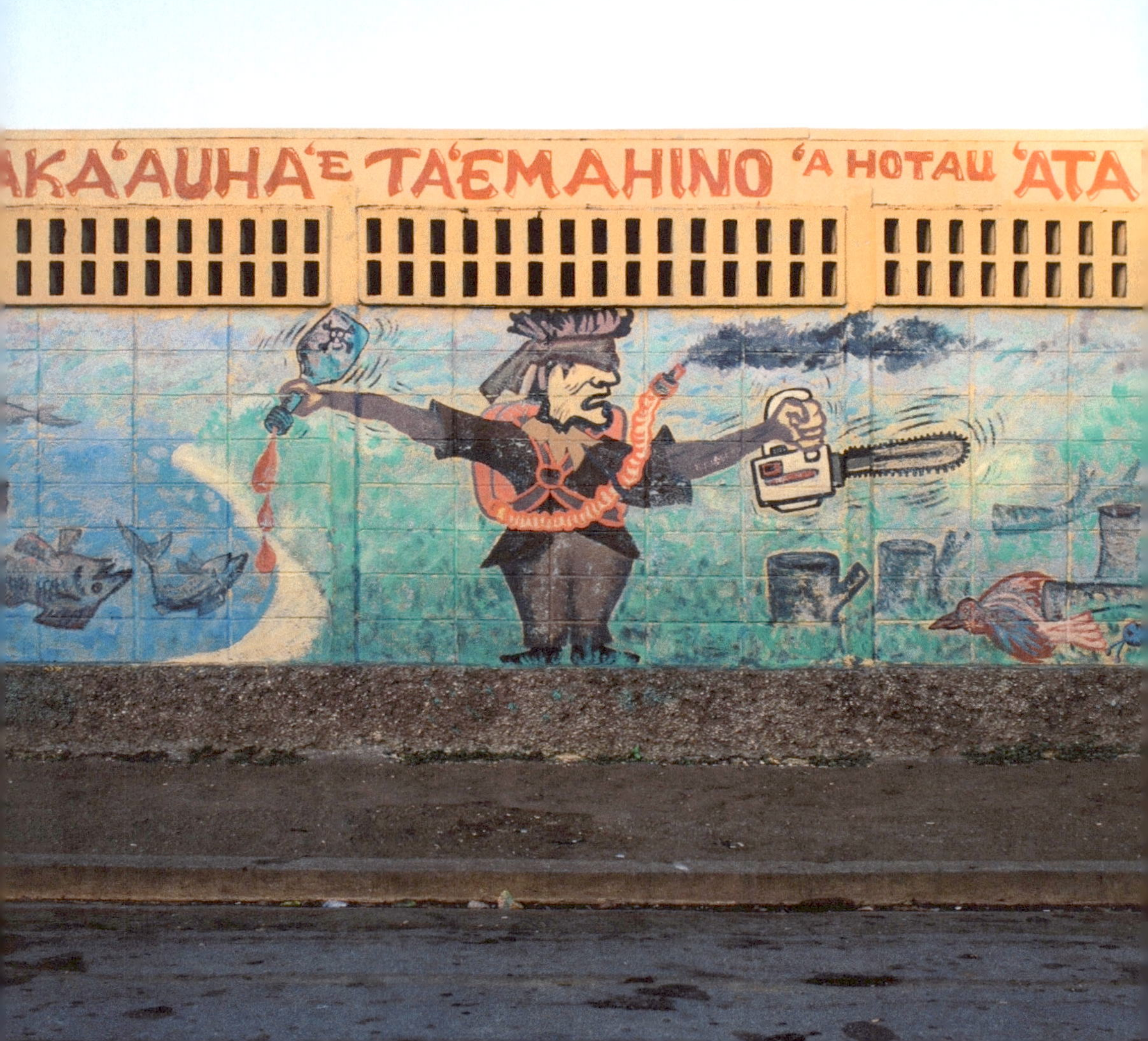
AKA‘AUHA ‘E TA‘EMAHINO ‘A HOTAU ‘ATA

Rising Seas, Preserving Paradise

Polynesia conveys images of pristine beauty and timeless isolation. In reality, the islands are fragile ecosystems, facing local environmental disturbances as well as challenges that originate in far distant industrial societies. Loss of natural habitat, alien plant and animal species, pollution, water salinity, and cyclones threaten both large and small islands. Rising seas and storm surges associated with climate change pose an existential threat to some low-lying atolls that in an extreme scenario are projected to disappear within a generation. On an early photography project in Samoa, I was enlisted to document a set of natural areas being preserved by local villagers. Their efforts led me to consider how cultural survival and the conservation of nature are mutually interdependent and how traditional knowledge can serve as a bridge to a more sustainable global future.

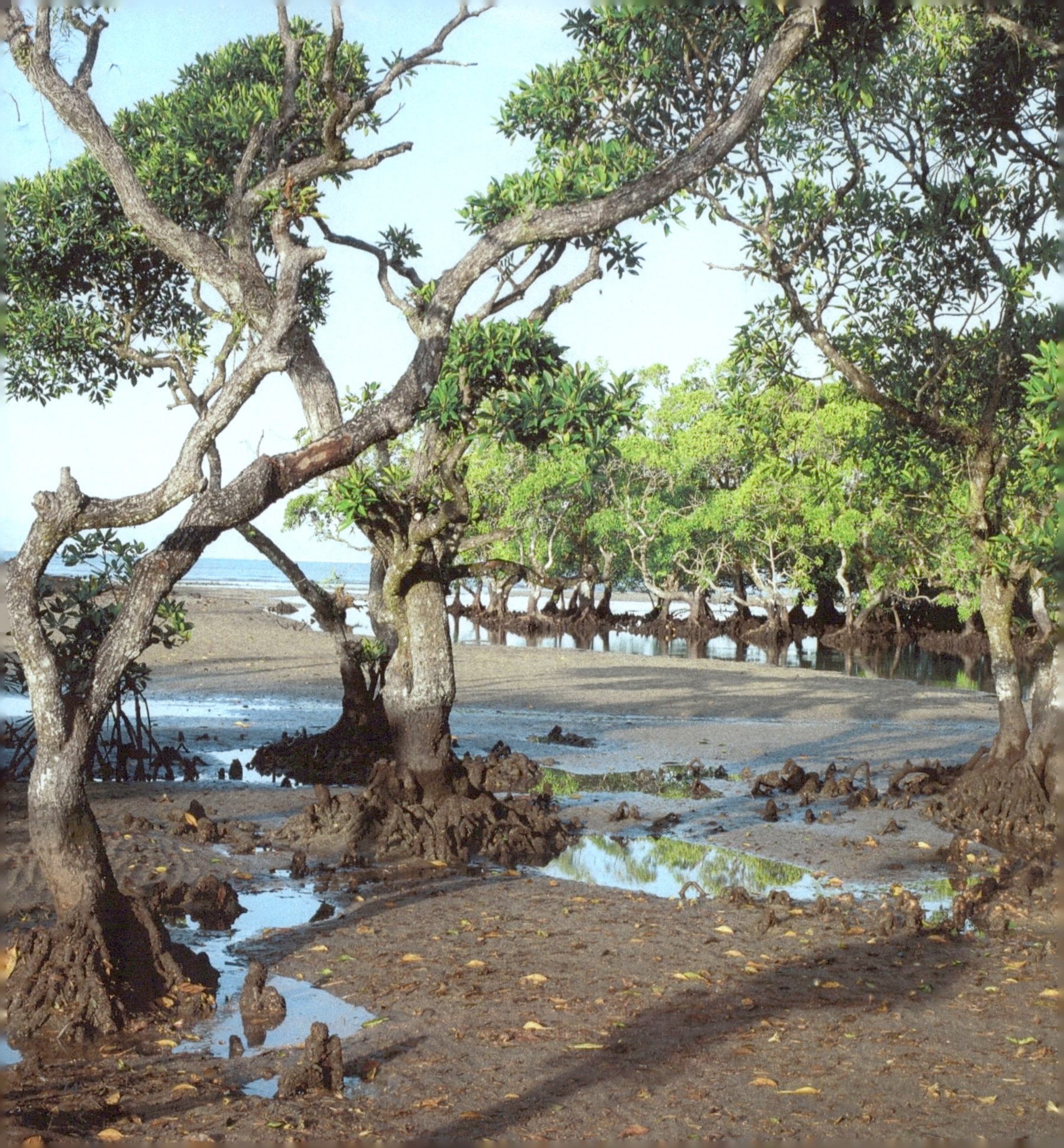

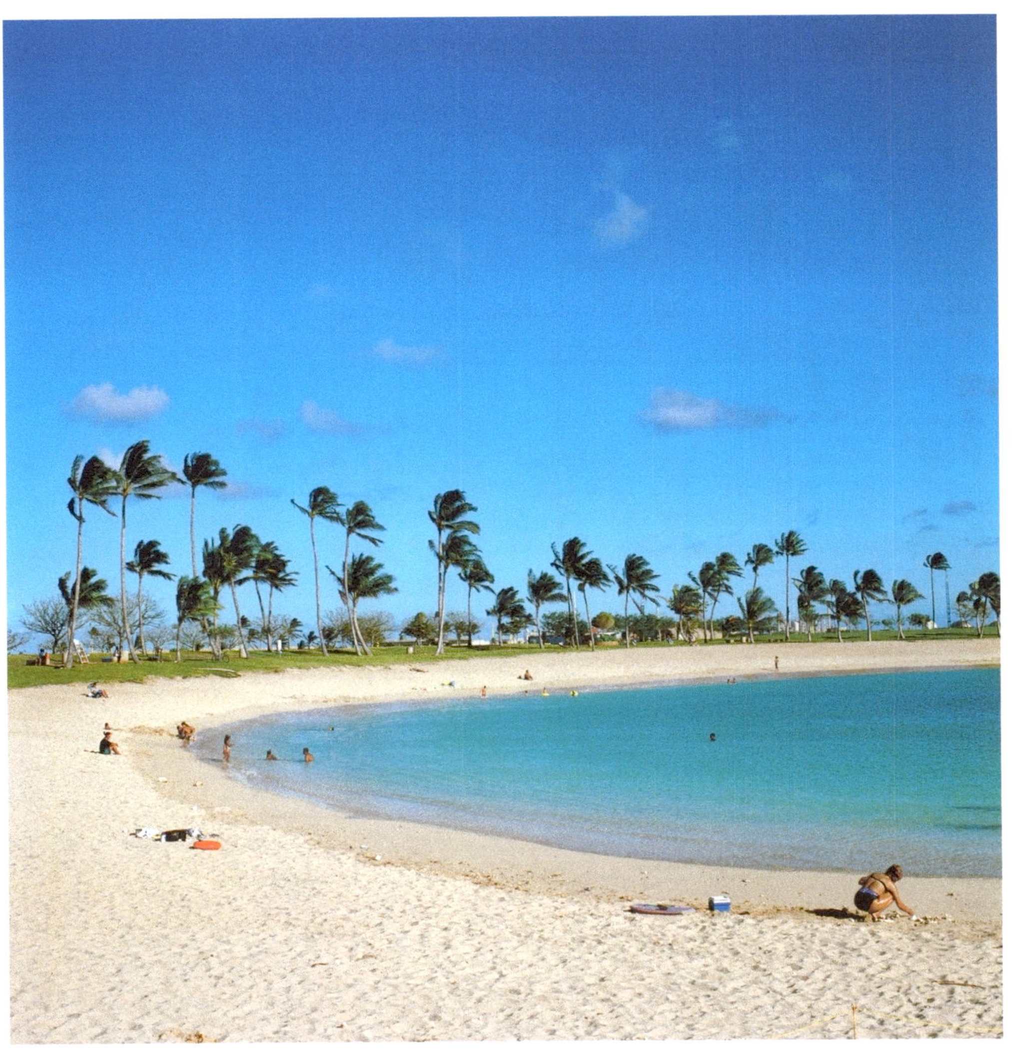

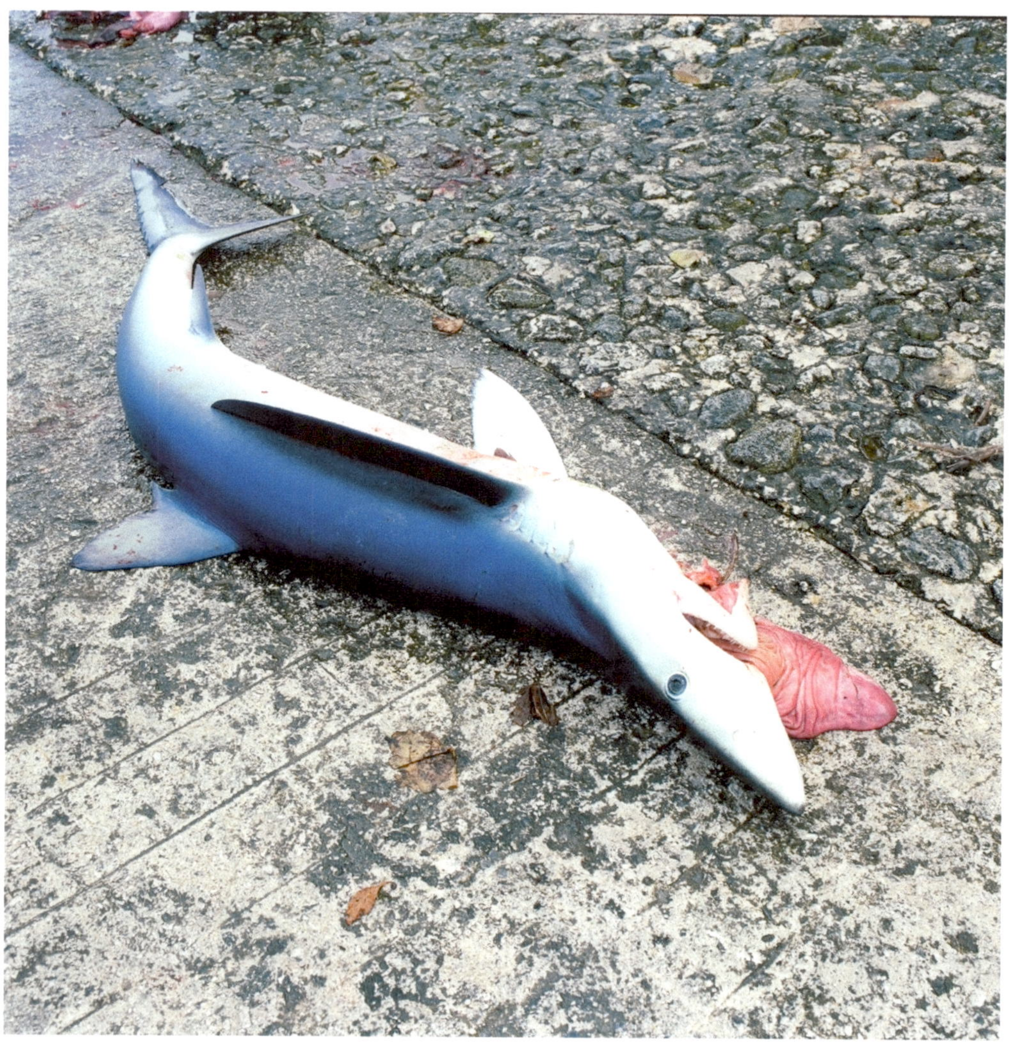

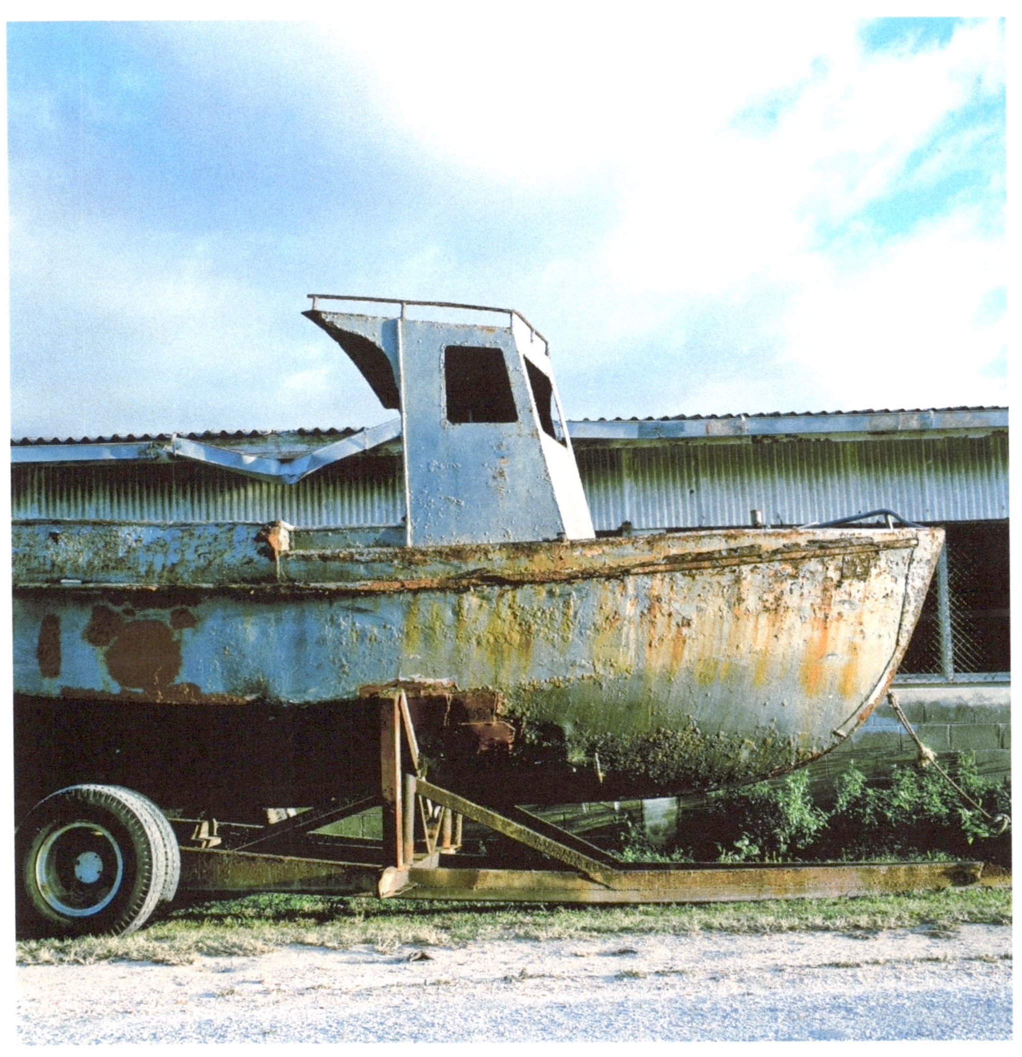

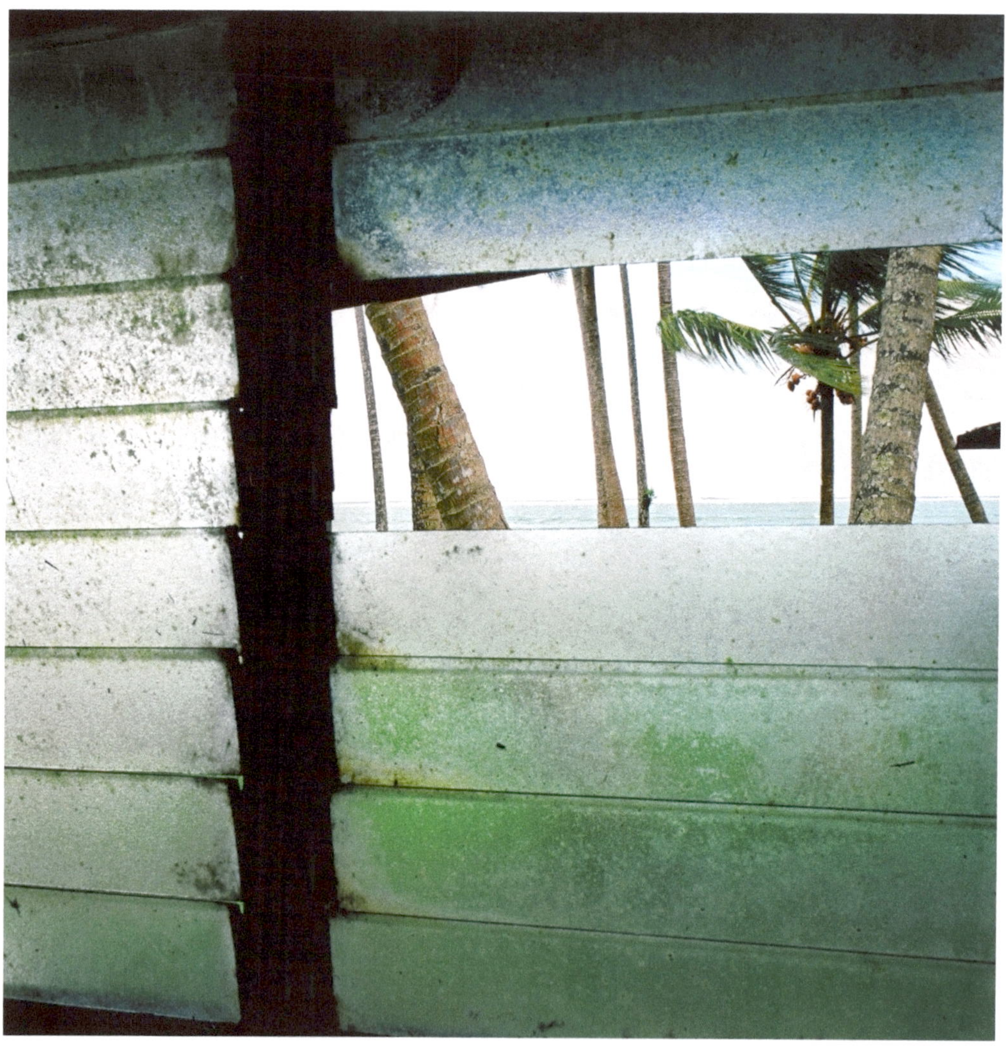

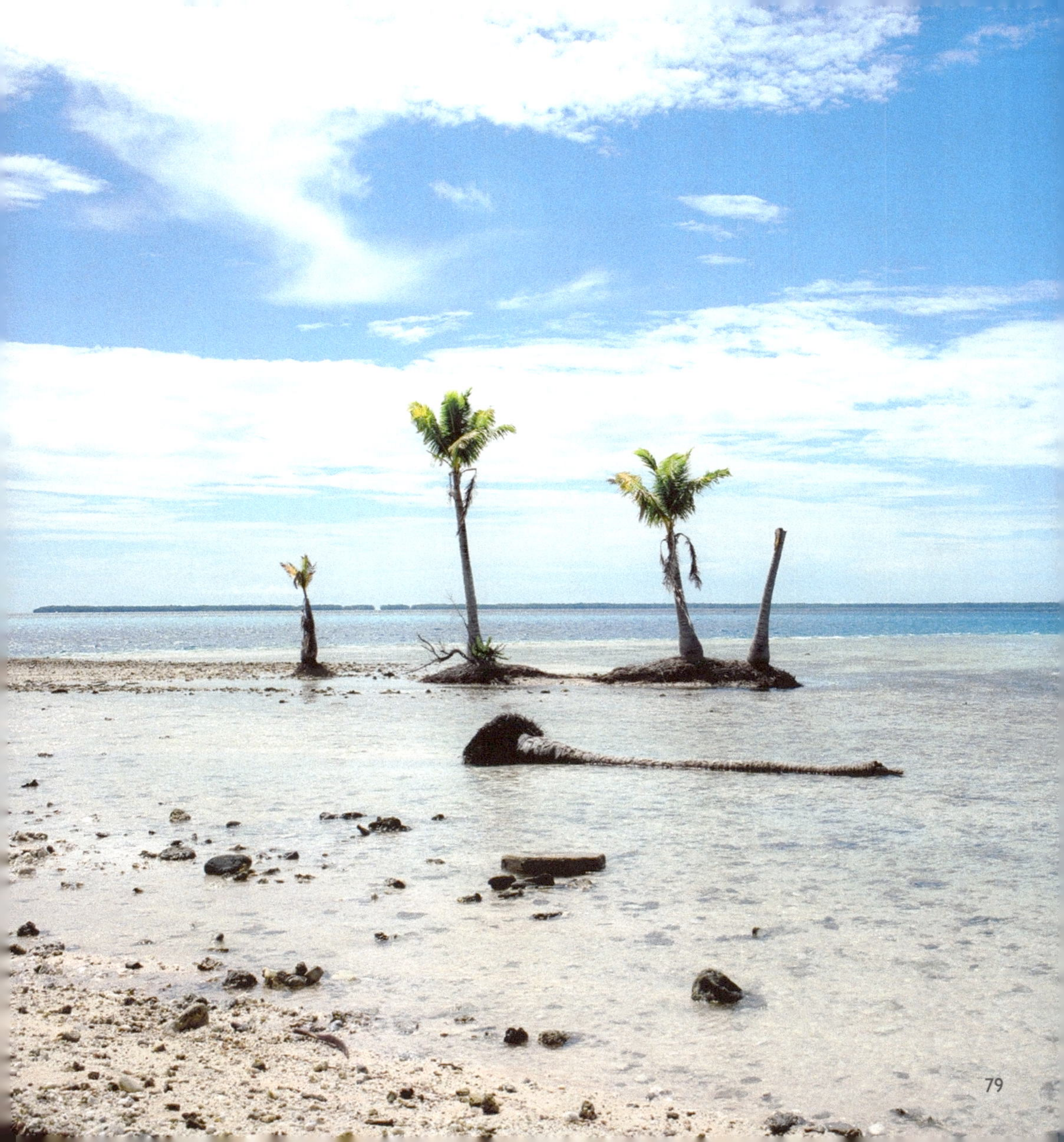

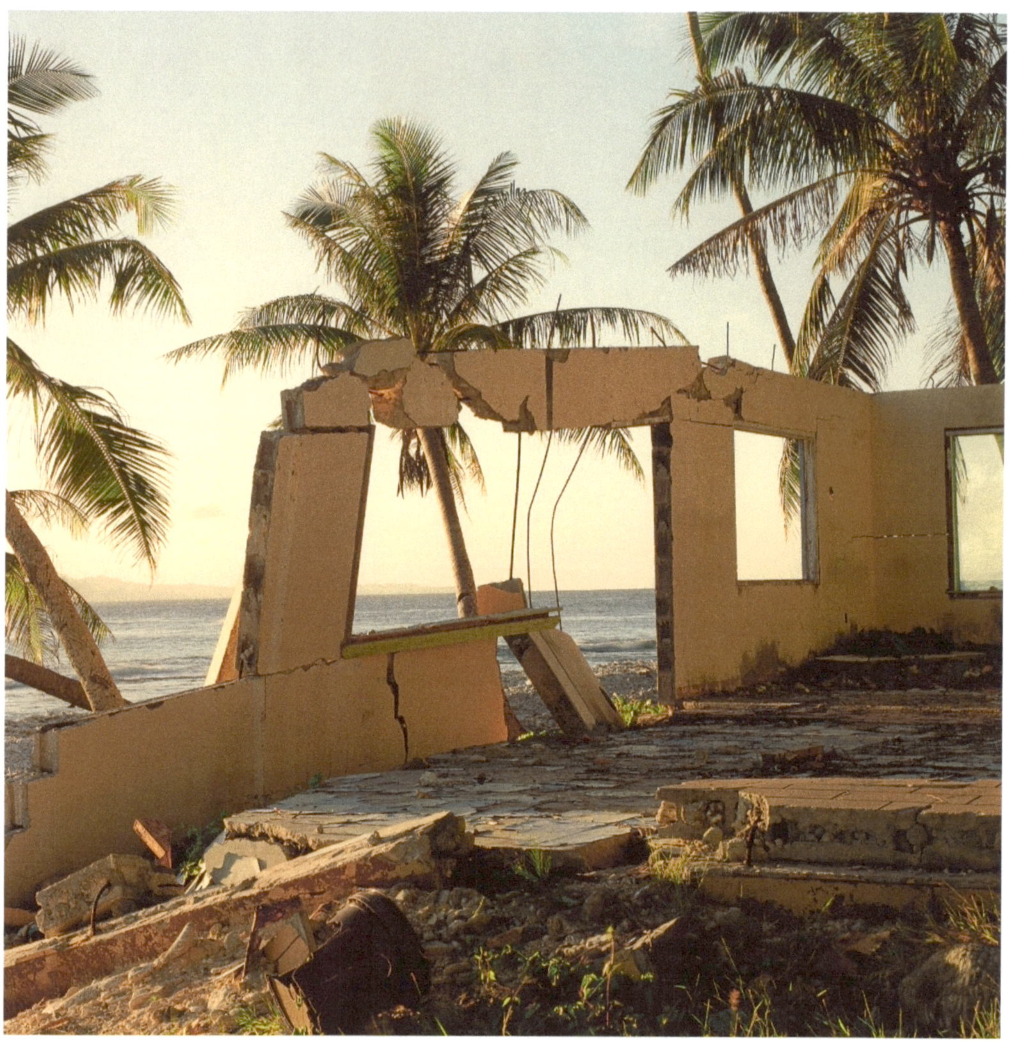

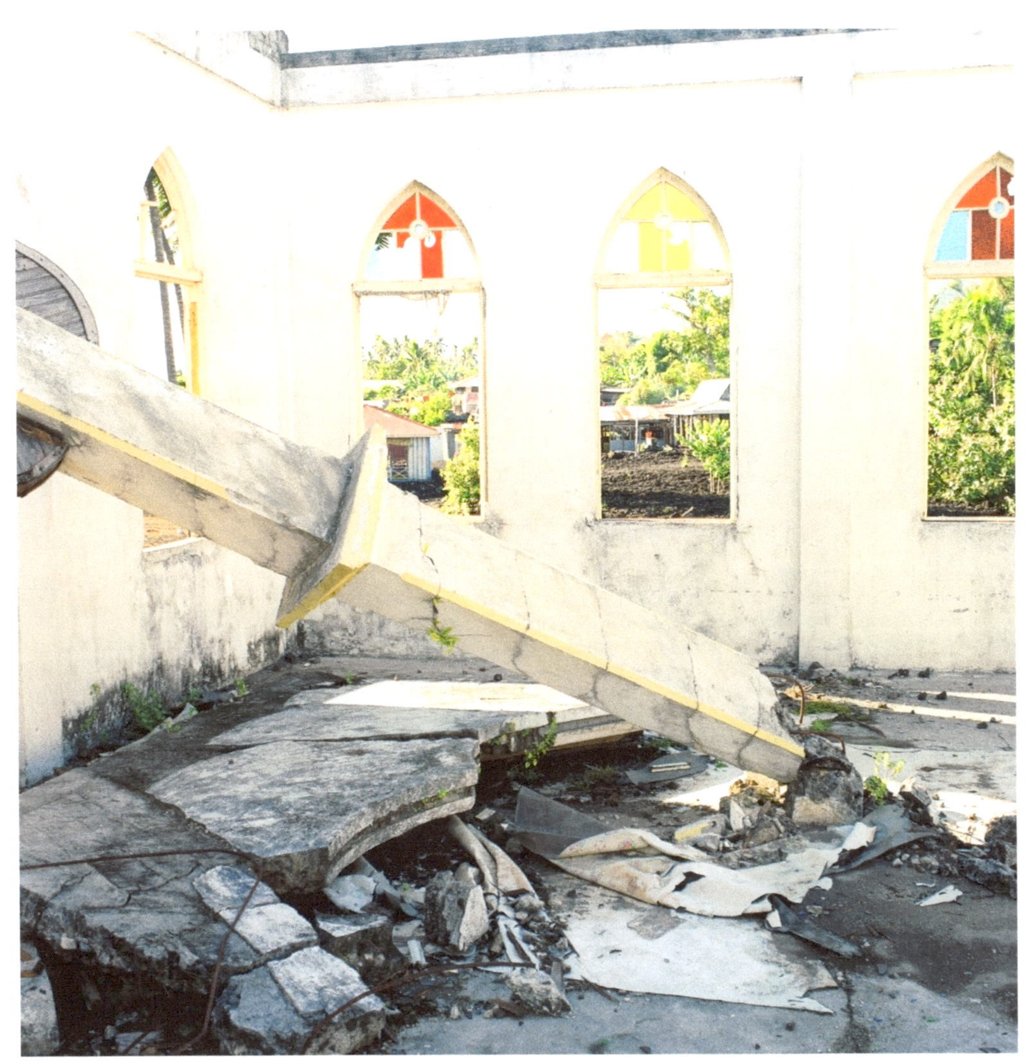

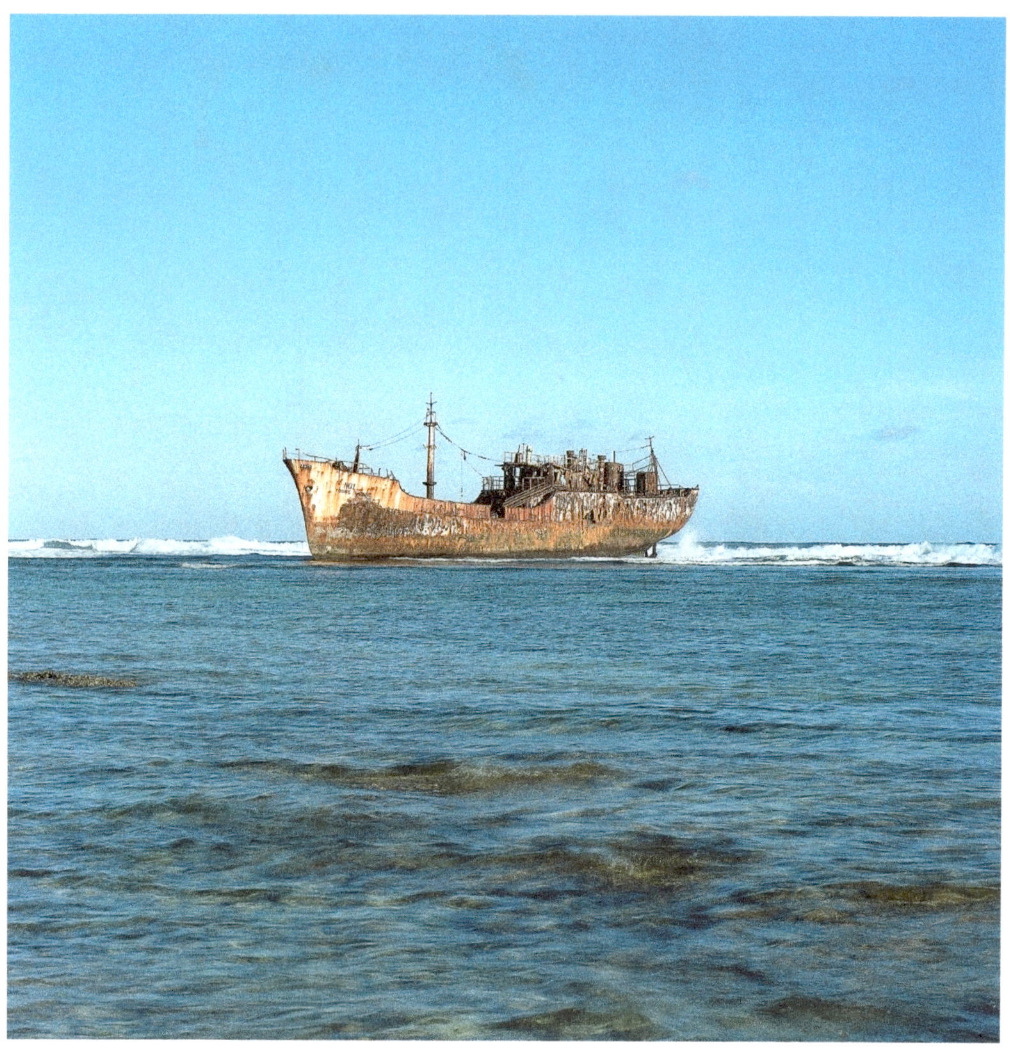

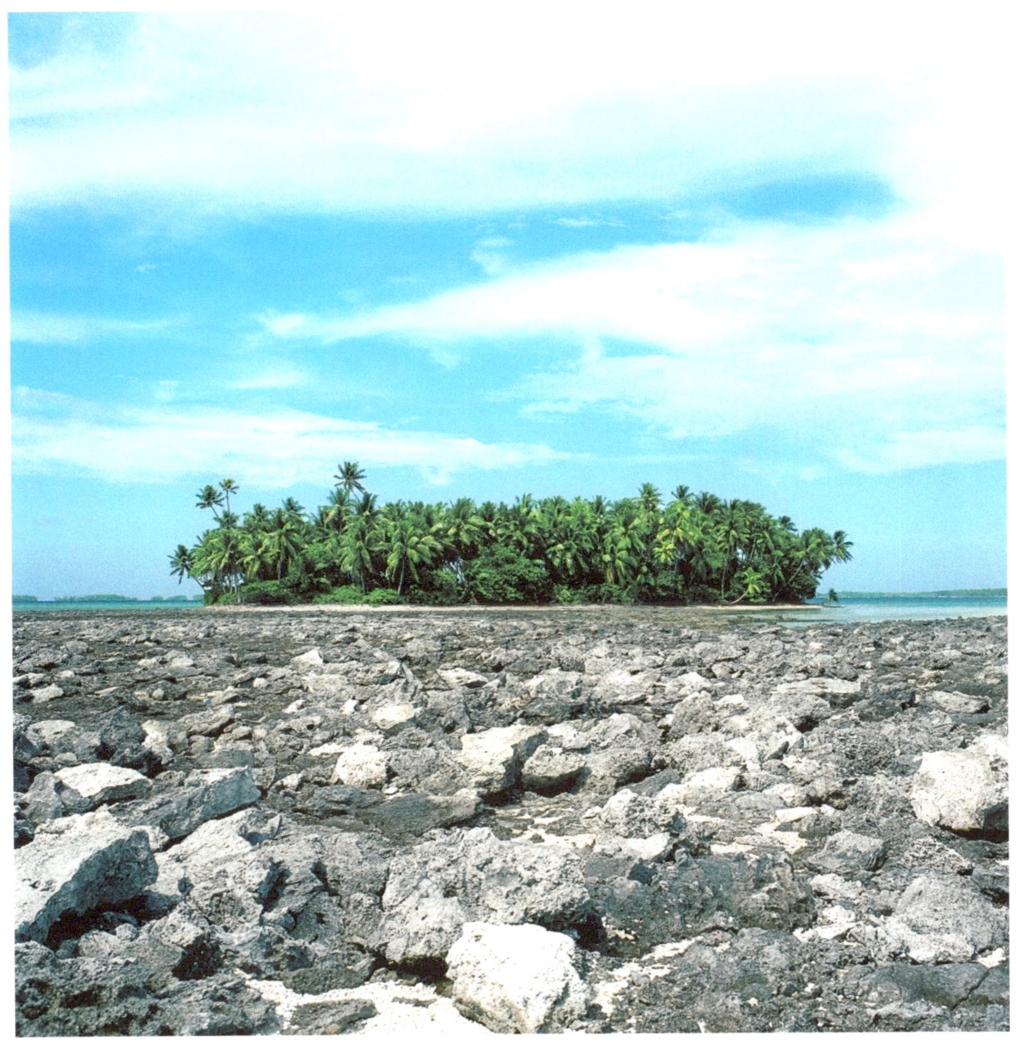

If we are forced to migrate because of climate change, our children will only look into a dream of what was.

—Preamble to National Climate Change Policy Framework, Republic of the Marshall Islands

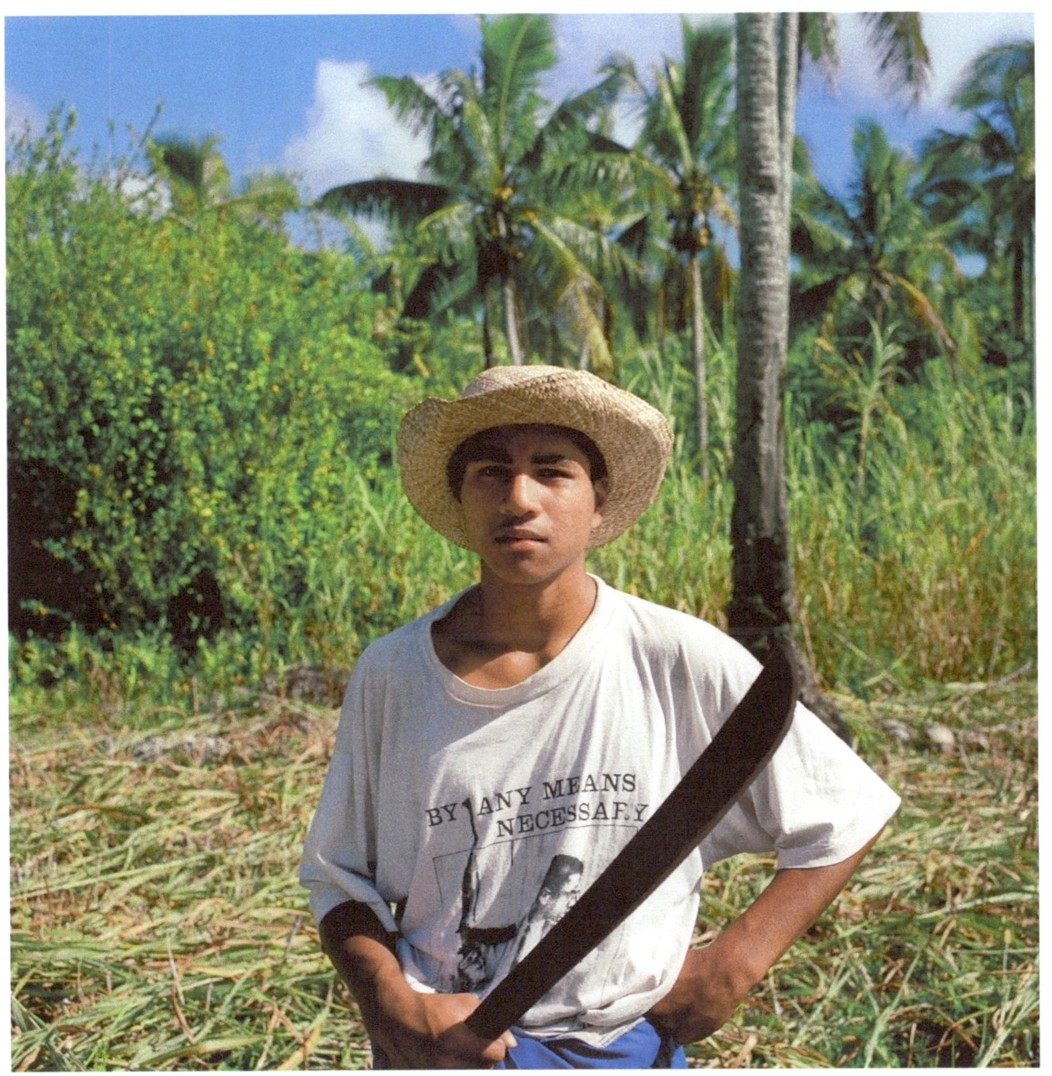
BY ANY MEANS
NECESSARY

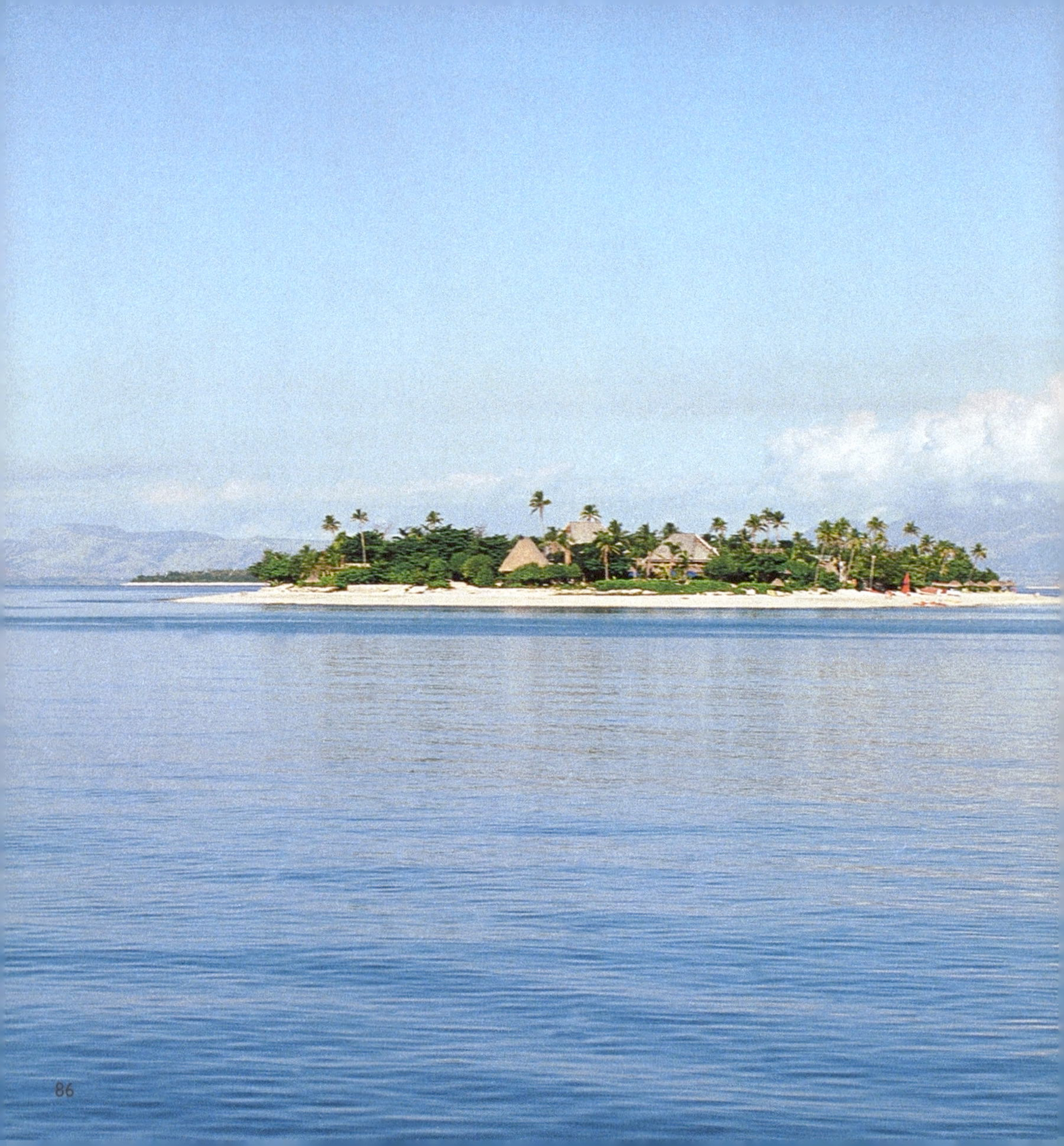

Island Life

There is no single scenario for contemporary life in Polynesia aside from that which has been erroneously foisted upon it by outsiders. The Hawaiians I know in Honolulu live worlds apart from the inhabitants of Samoa's upland rainforests or Tokelau's coral islets. Yet they share a past and face a similar uncertain future. Tourism, resources, and politics play key roles in the development of island society, but so, too, do environmental knowledge, individual aspirations, and culture. As Polynesia becomes ever more entangled with the world at large, its inhabitants face a daunting task: to look to the past for strength and wisdom but to the future for opportunities, and to do so without unduly sacrificing cultural heritages or natural settings. In this regard, their challenge is shared by all people living everywhere on the island of Earth.

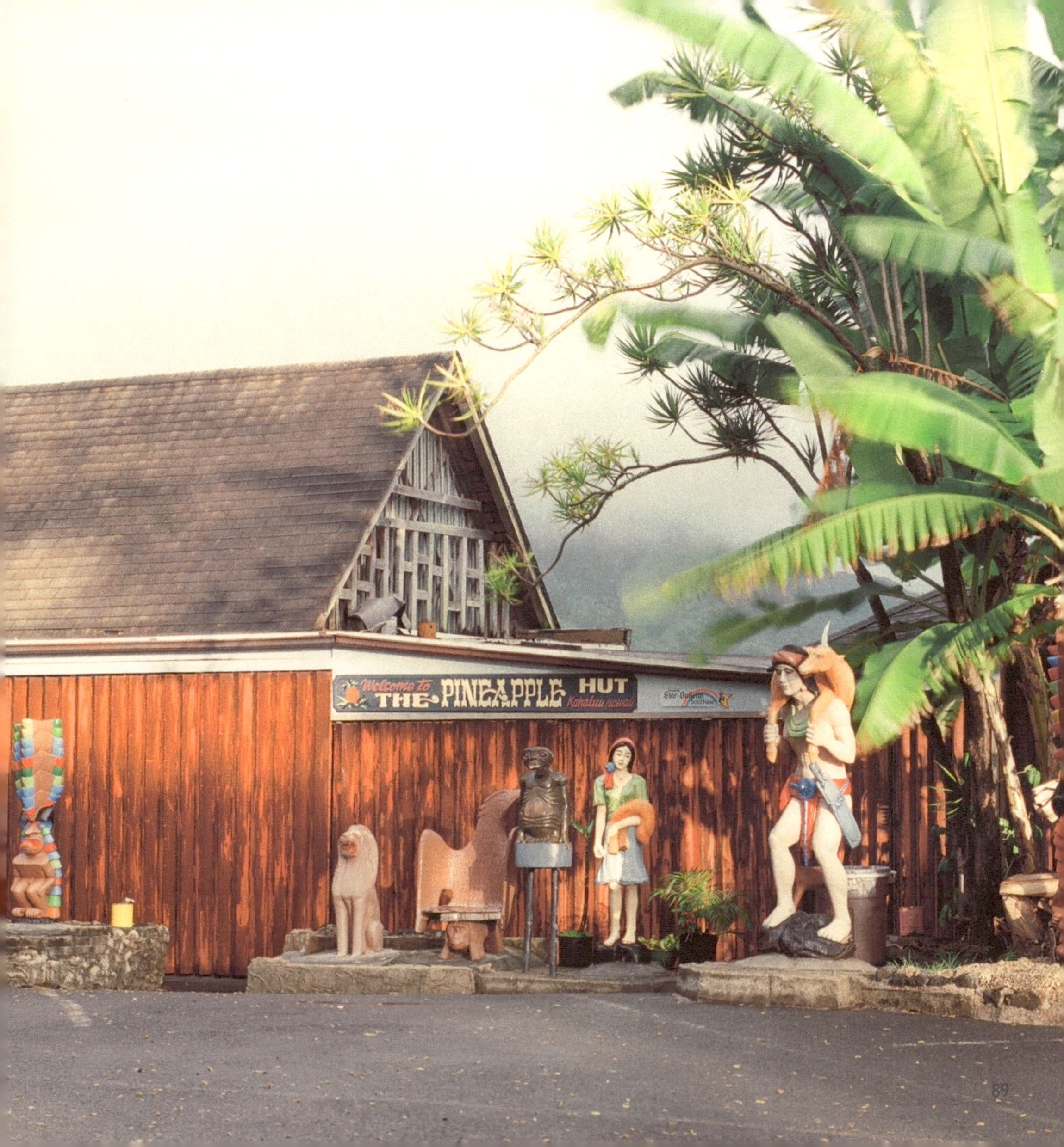
Welcome to
THE PINEAPPLE HUT
Kahaluu Hawaii
Star-Bulletin
Sold Here

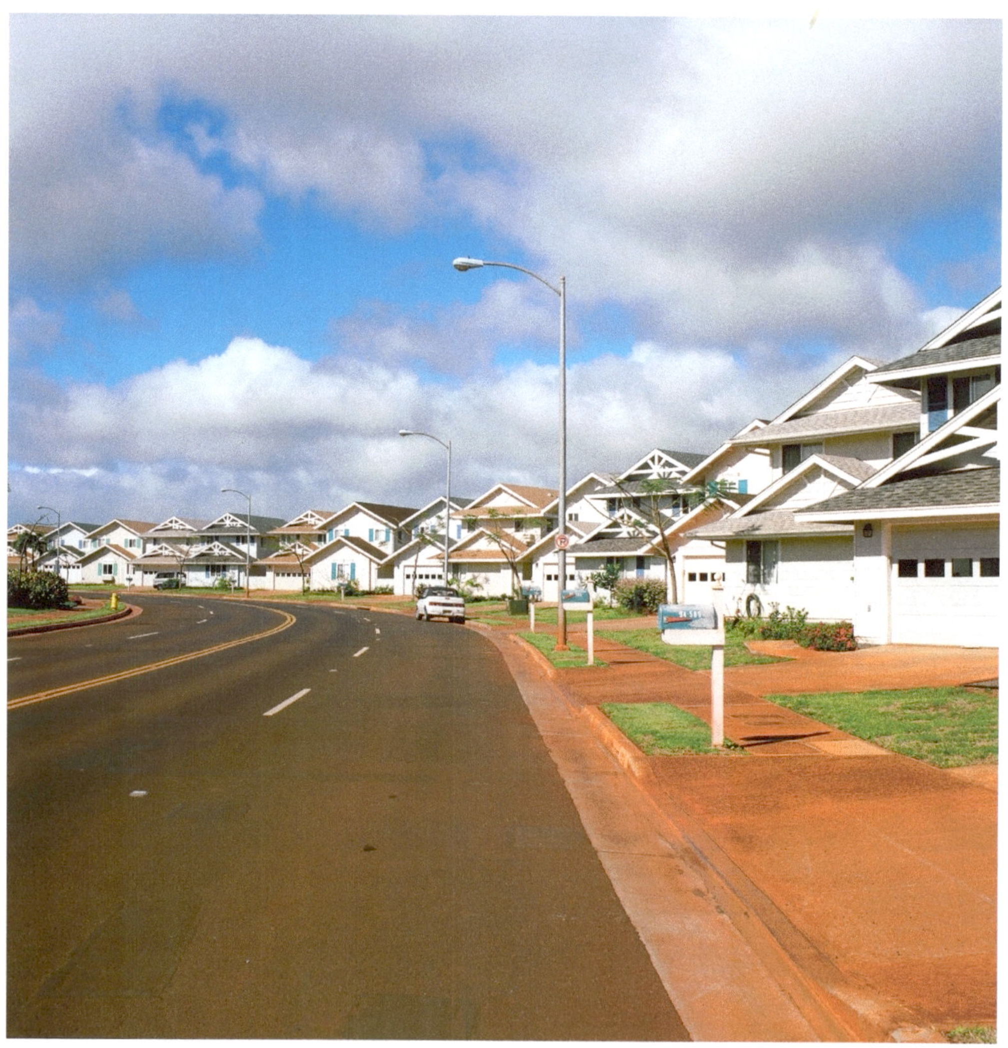

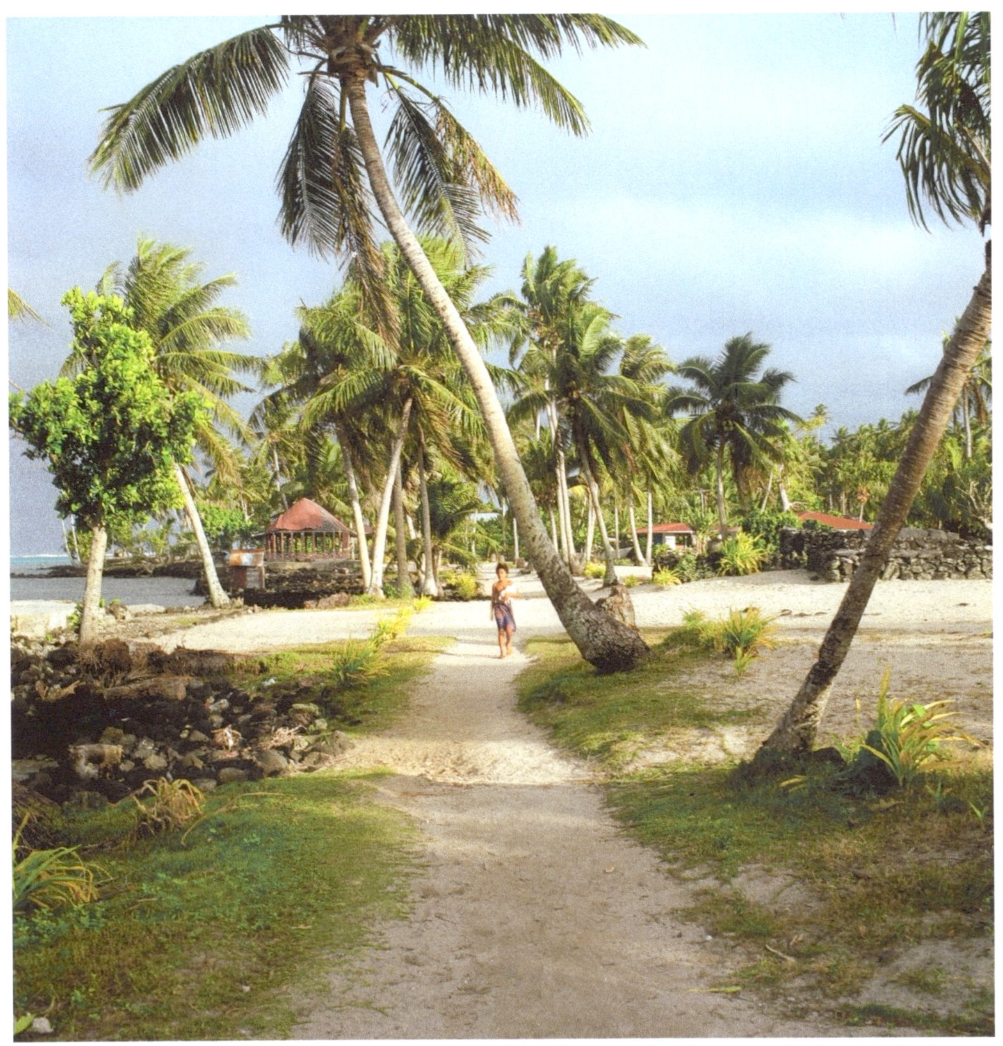

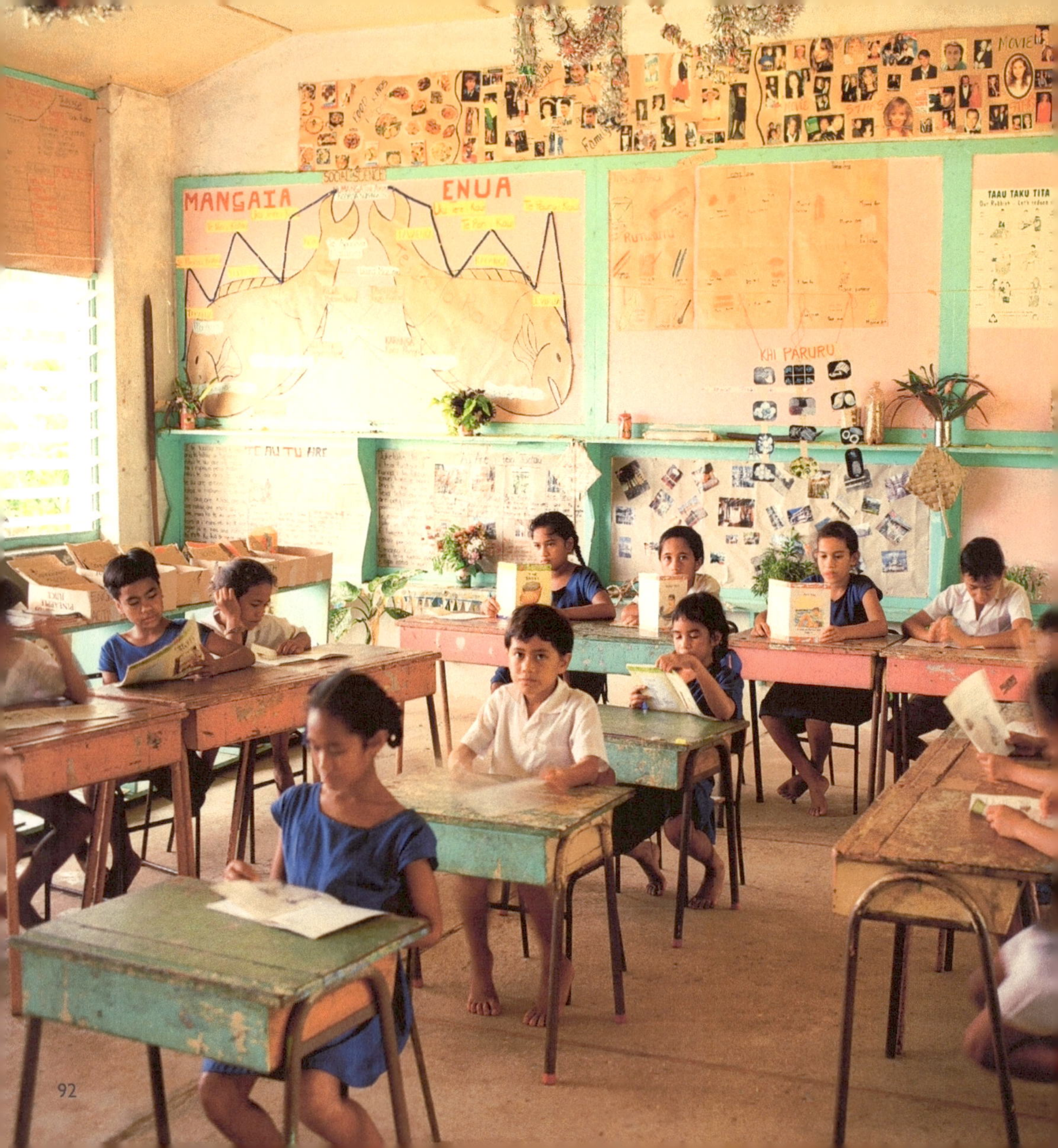
MANGAIA
ENUA
KAI PARURU
TAAU TAKU TITA

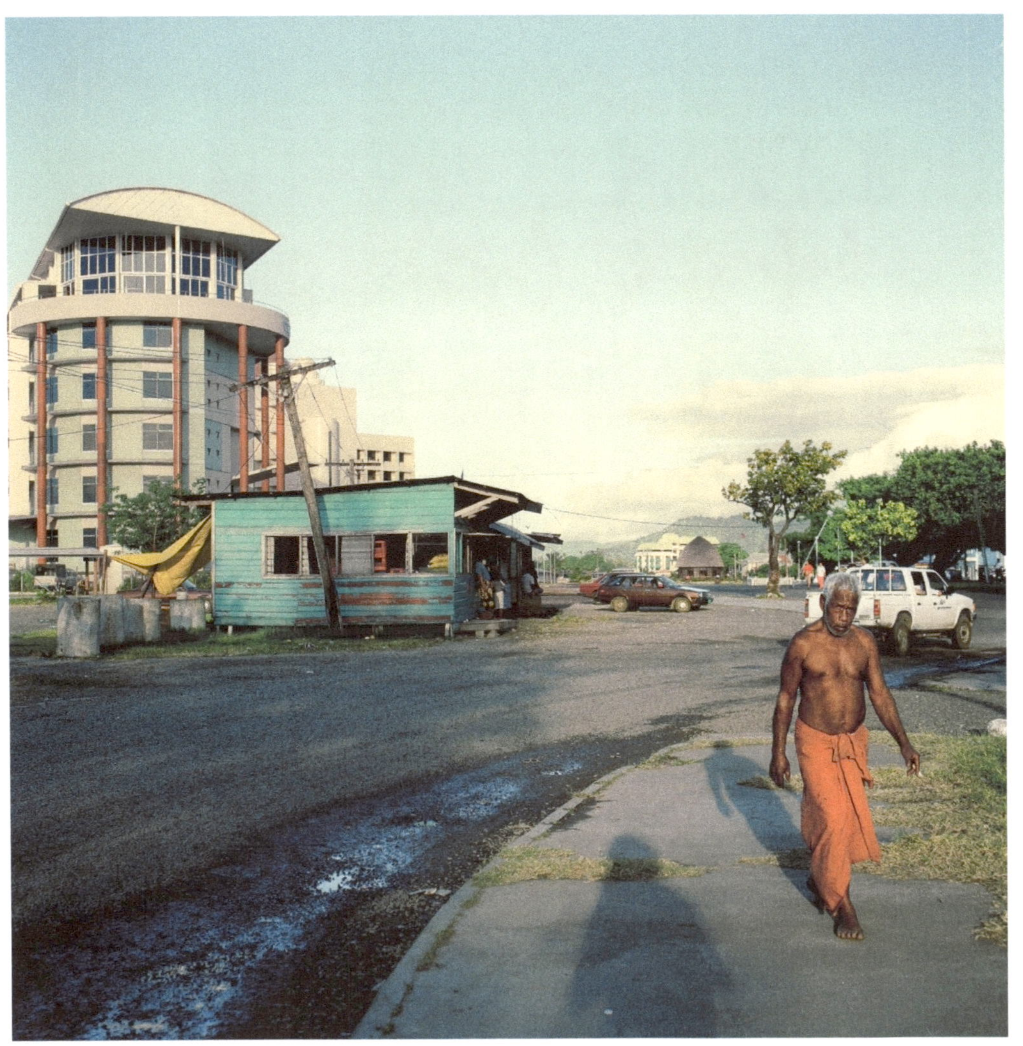

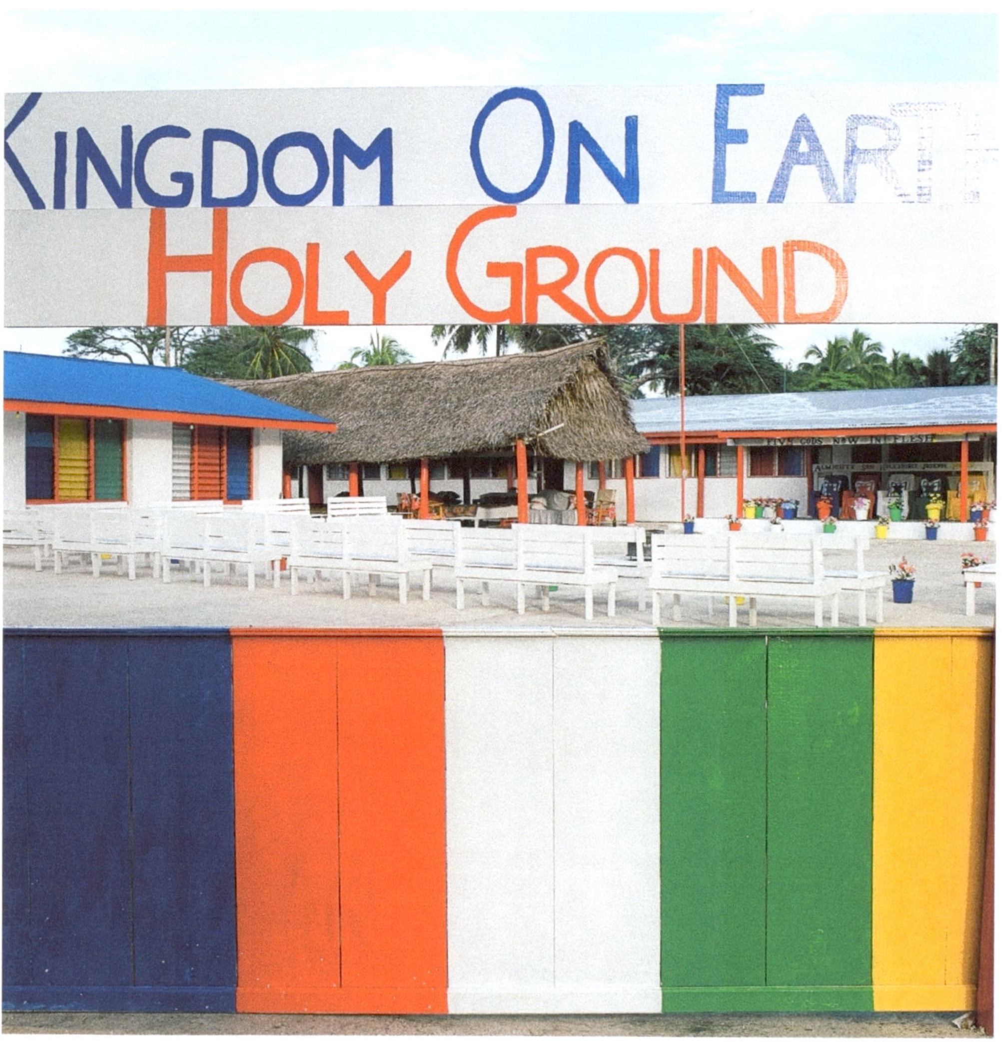
KINGDOM ON EART
HOLY GROUND

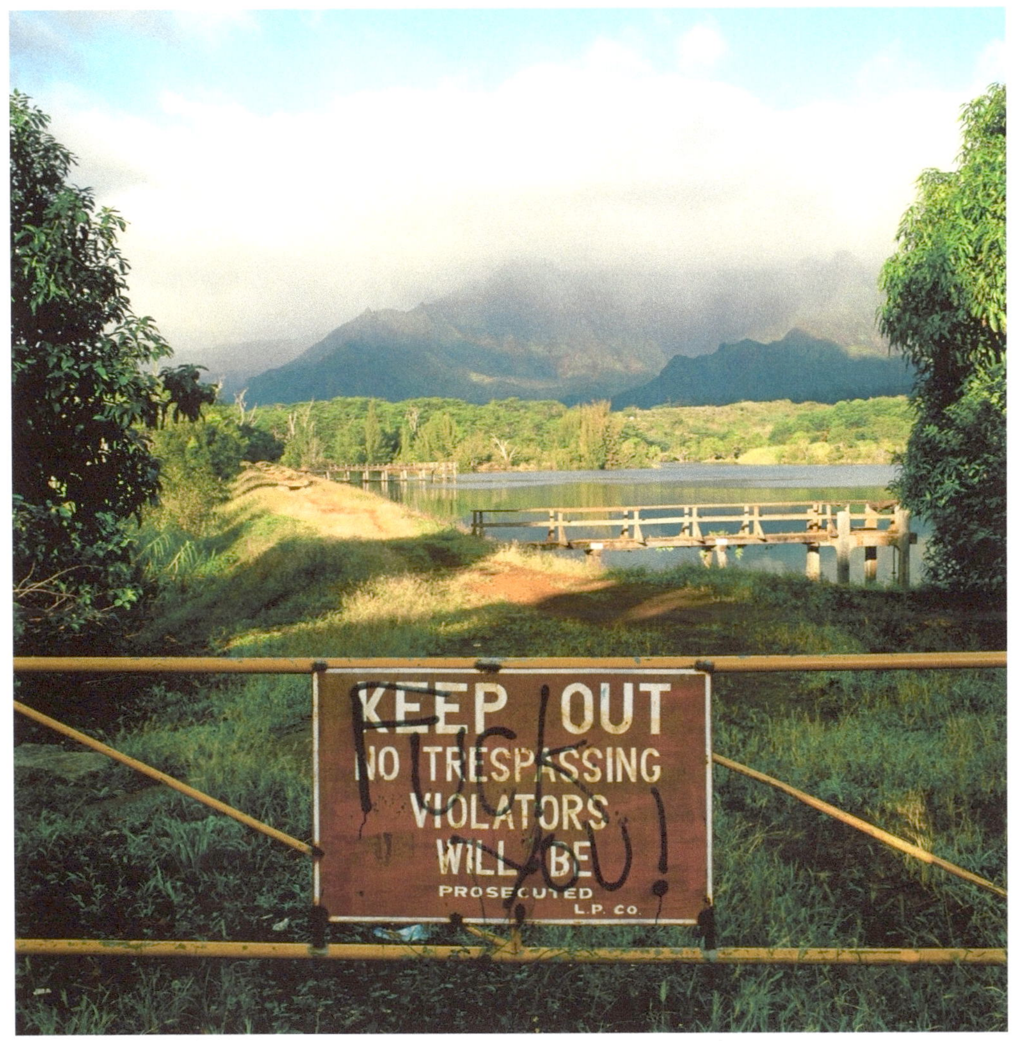
KEEP OUT
NO TRESPASSING
VIOLATORS
WILL BE
PROSECUTED
L.P. Co.
FUCK YOU!

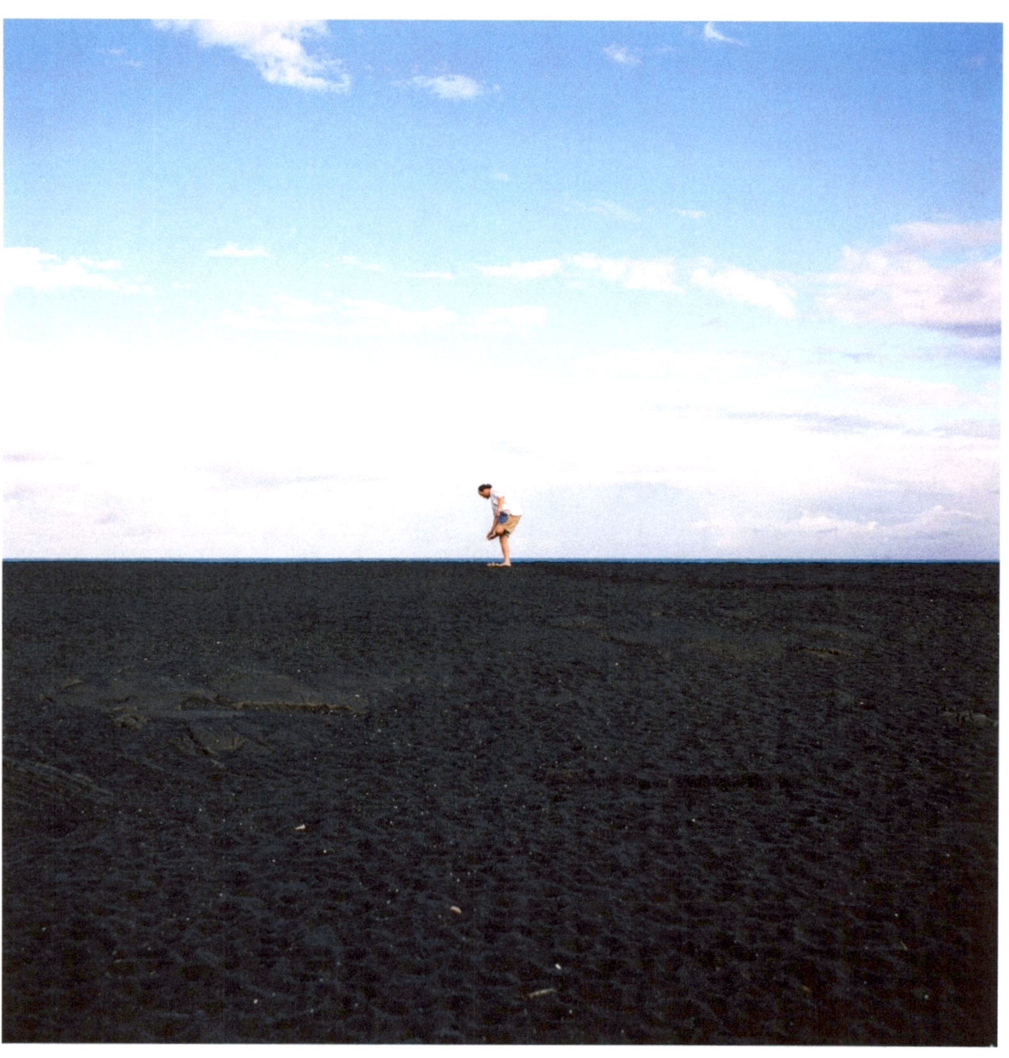

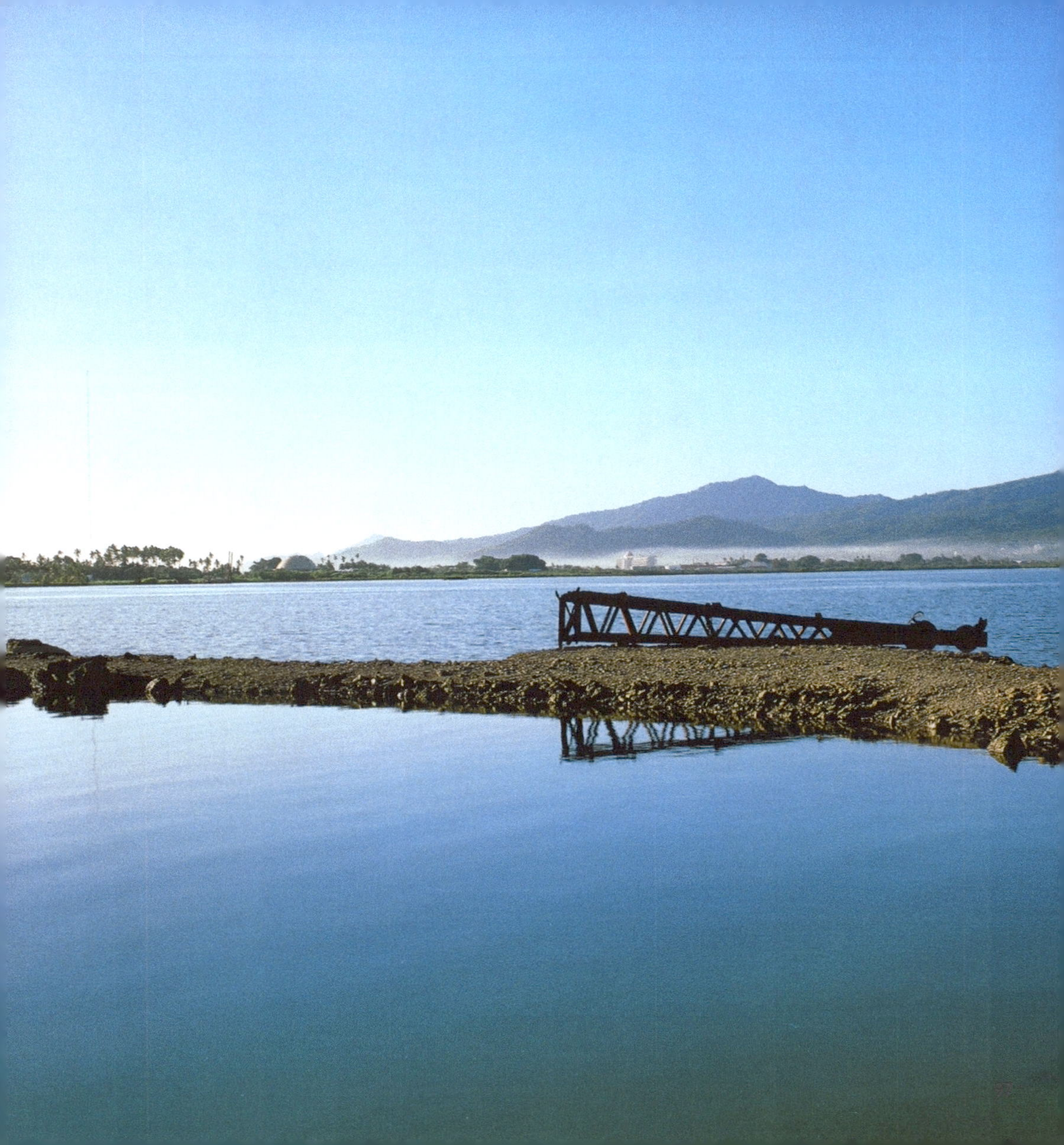

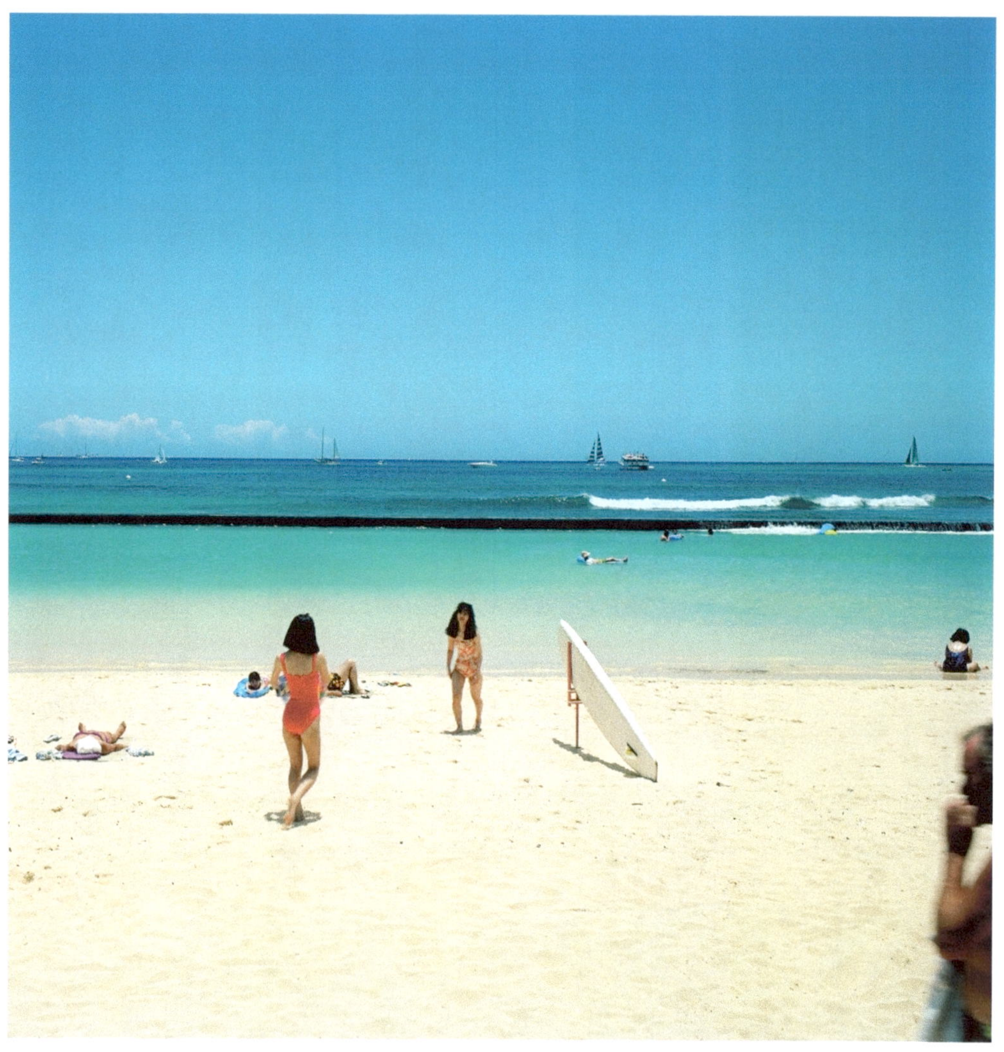

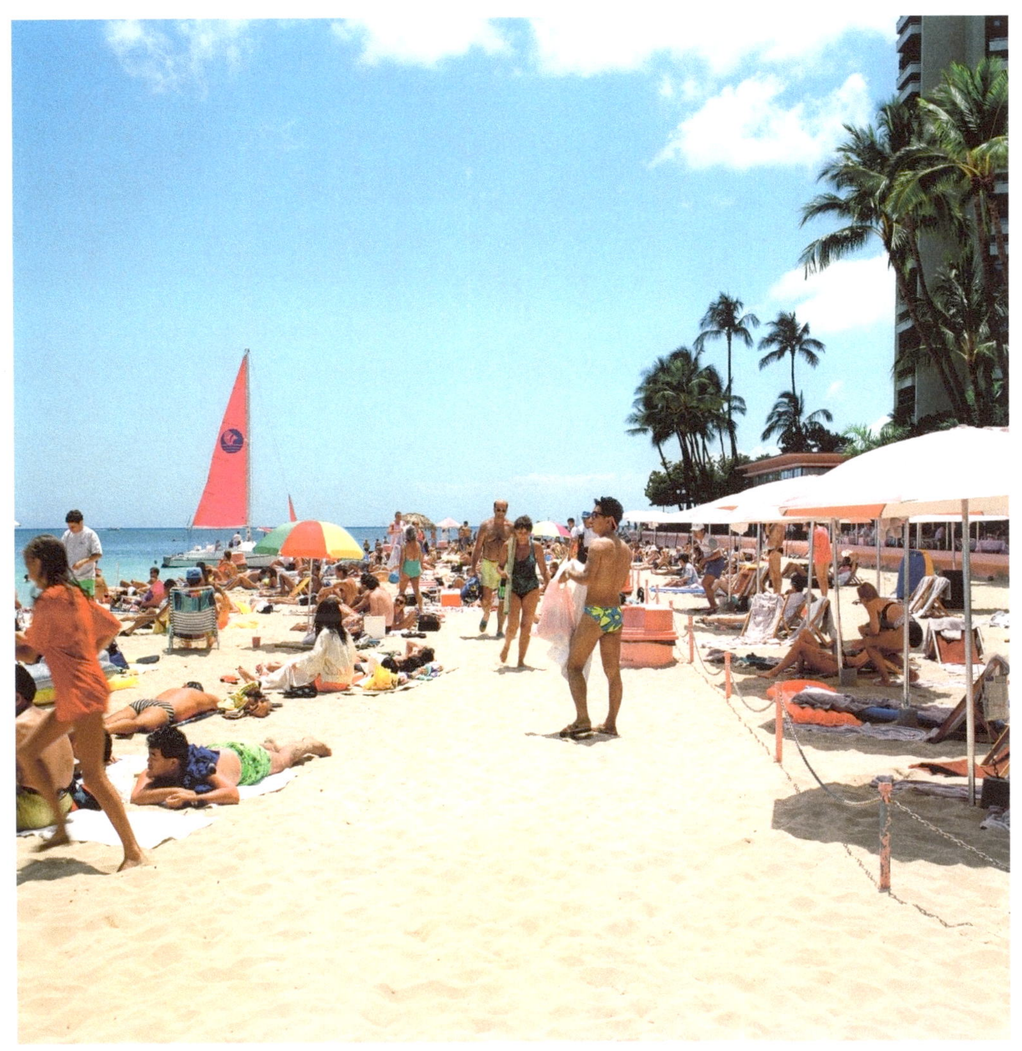

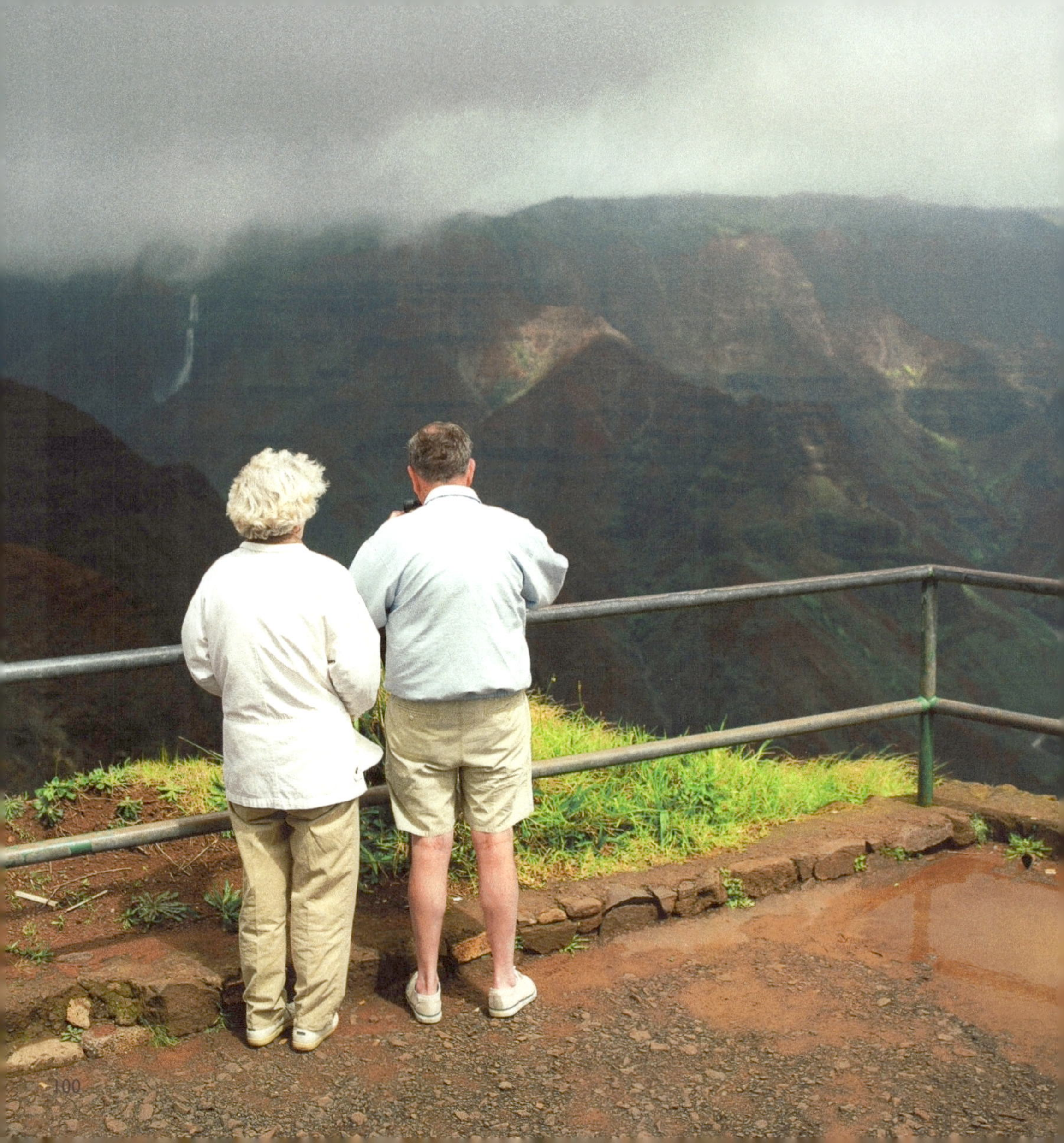

Whispering ghost of the west,
Who brought you here
To our land?
Stand up and depart!

—Traditional Polynesian chant

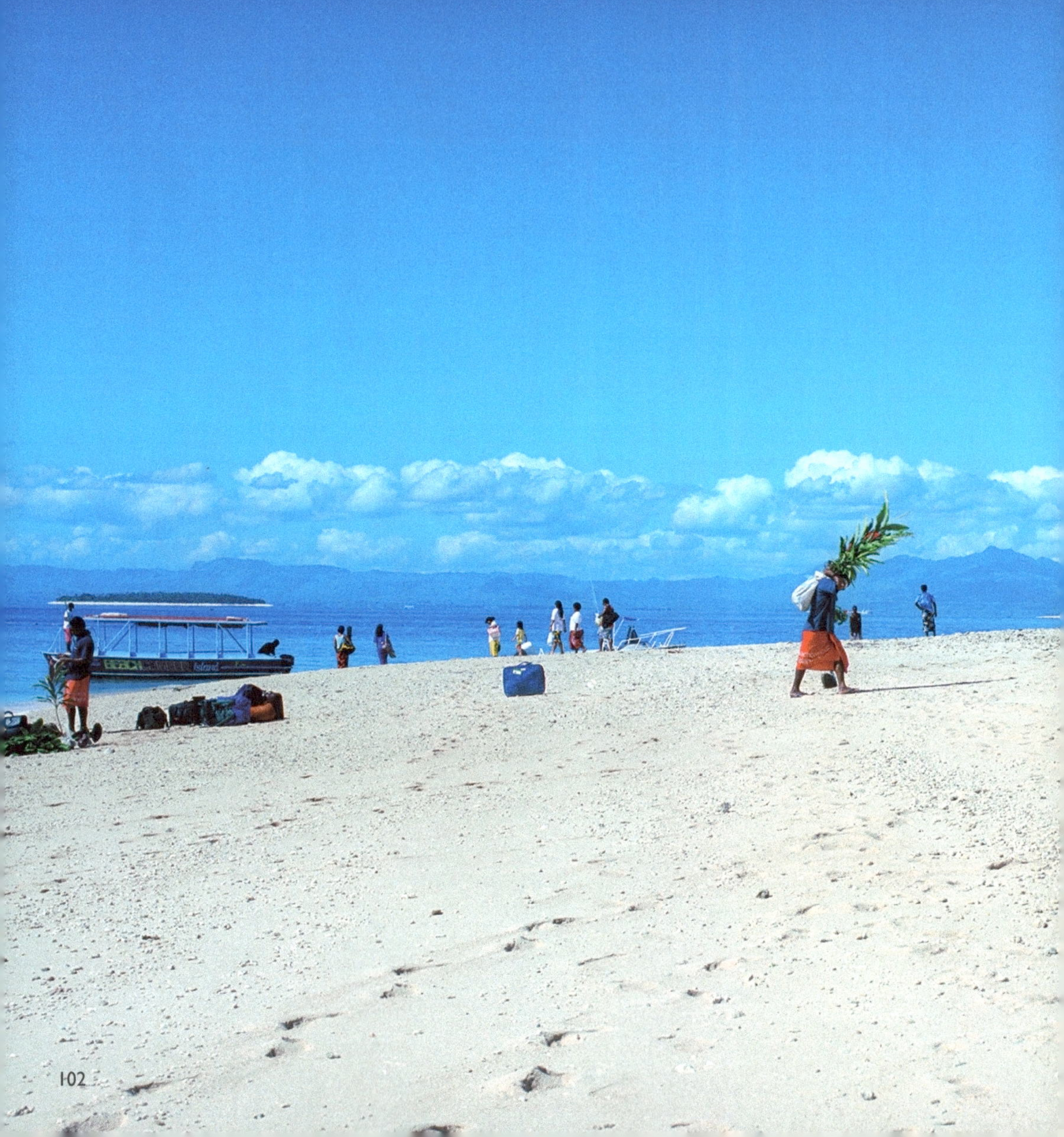

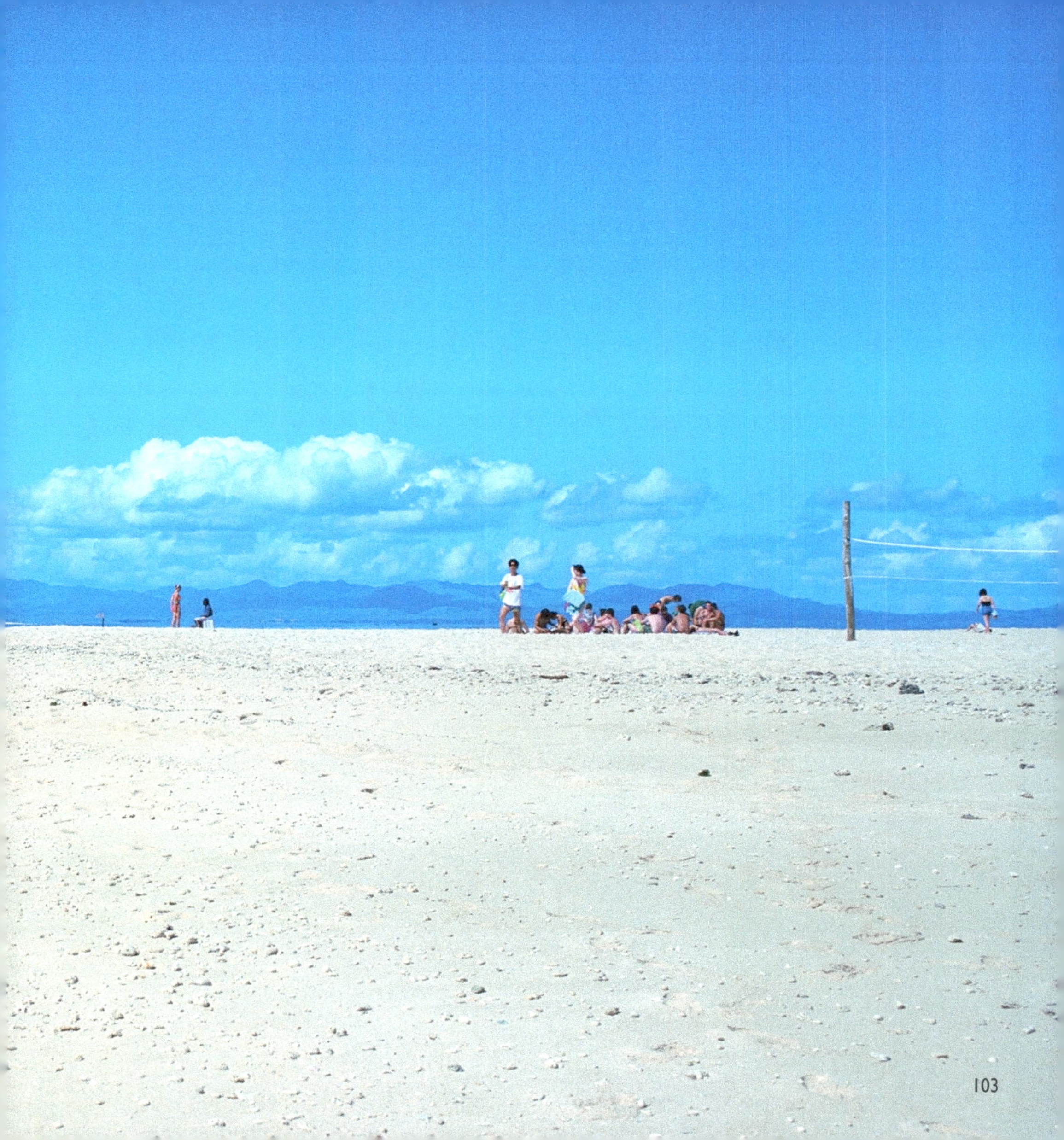

Acknowledgments

A big thank you to the Ala'ilima family, and in memory of Leiataua Vaiao and Fay Ala'ilima, who did so much to advance the cause of Pacific Islanders.

I am grateful to the O le Siosiomaga Society (Apia) for providing a substantial grant in early years to complete a body of photographic work on protected natural areas in Samoa.

Thank you East-West Center (Honolulu) for providing a fellowship, an education, a community of like-minded souls, and a vibrant home in Hawaii.

Thank you Alan Marcus for writing the book foreword.

Thank you Dan Silvestri at Impact Photo for expert assistance with the negative scans and related lab work on photographs.

Thank you Doug Zurick for painting the map.

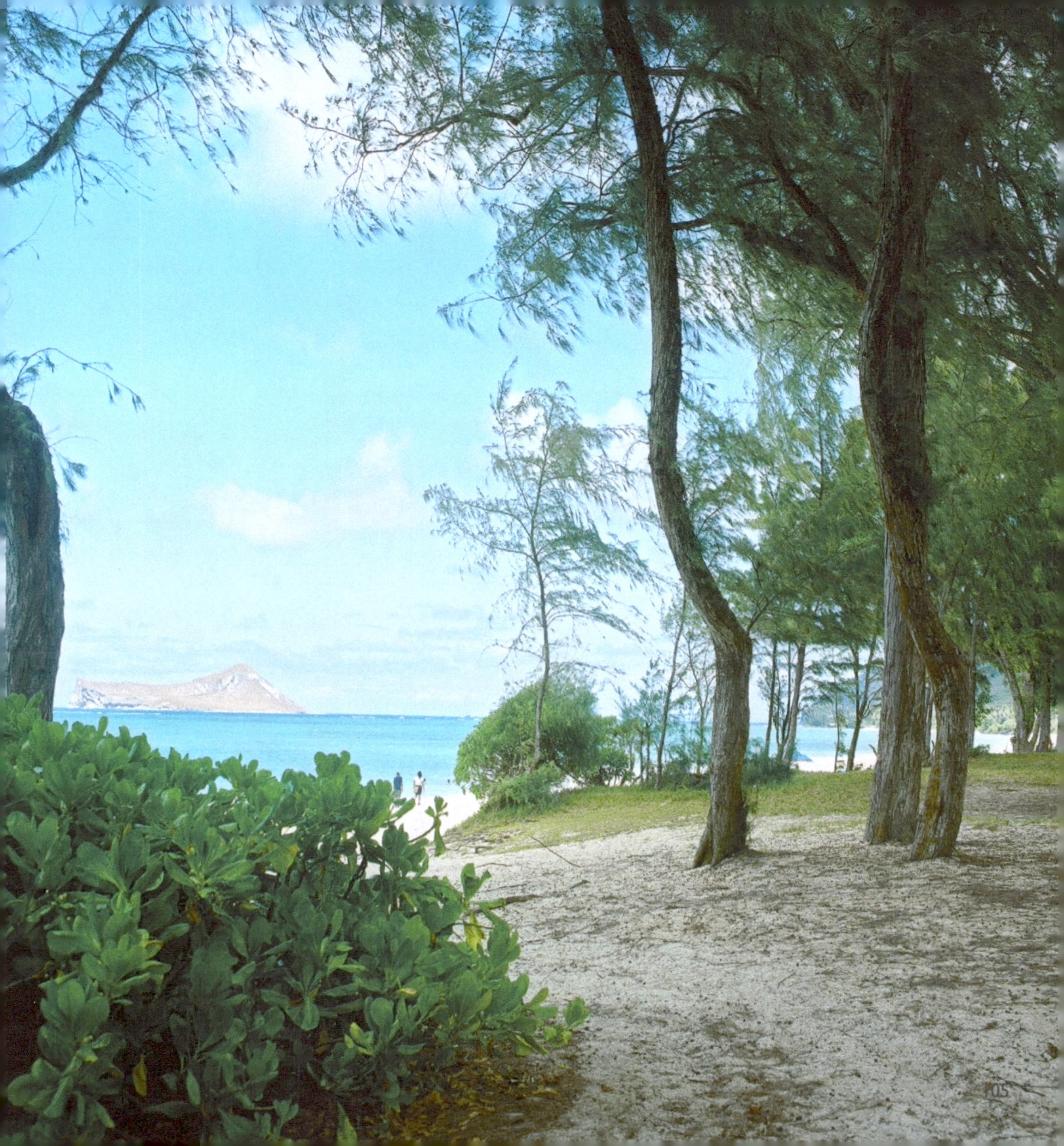

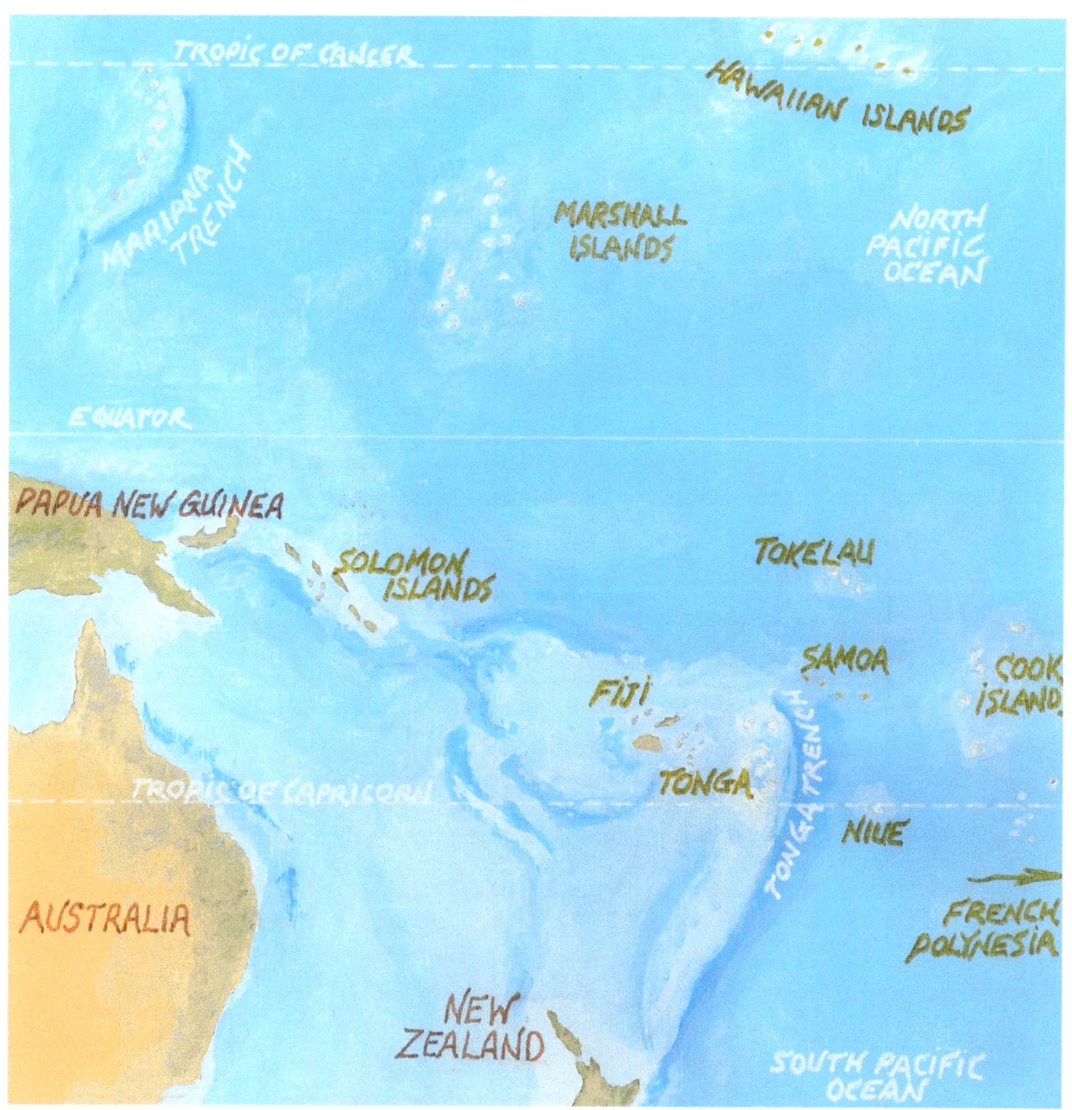
TROPIC OF CANCER
HAWAIIAN ISLANDS
MARIANA TRENCH
MARSHALL ISLANDS
NORTH PACIFIC OCEAN
EQUATOR
PAPUA NEW GUINEA
SOLOMON ISLANDS
TOKELAU
SAMOA
COOK ISLANDS
FIJI
TONGA TRENCH
TONGA
TROPIC OF CAPRICORN
NIUE
FRENCH POLYNESIA
AUSTRALIA
NEW ZEALAND
SOUTH PACIFIC OCEAN

Note on Geography

Polynesia encompasses a triangle of oceanic space in the central and southern Pacific Ocean, with Hawaii at its apex and Aotearoa (New Zealand) and Rapa Nui (Easter Island) at its base. Within this vast realm live an estimated three million people who self-identify as Polynesians. The map that appears on the facing page contains places covered in the book's photography; it is not a complete coverage of Polynesia.

Guide to Photographs

American Samoa, Tutuila Island	page 82
Cook Islands, Mangaia Island	pages 54–55, 56, 57, 59, 66, 77, 92
Cook Islands, Rarotonga	pages 48, 60, 61
Fiji, Sigatoka	pages 86–87
Fiji, Viti Levu, Sigatoka Dunes	page 53
Hawaii, Hawaii Island	pages 21 (lava flow), 25, 29, 34–35, 96
Hawaii, Kauai Island	pages 28, 45 (taro, introduced food plant), 95, 100
Hawaii, Oahu Island	pages 16, 41 (botanical park), 42 (heliconia, introduced species), 43 (ti, native species), 46 & 47 (introduced desert botanicals), 67, 68, 75 (man-made beach), 89, 90, 98 & 99 (Waikiki Beach), 105
Koro Sea, Tourist Island	pages 102–103
Niue	pages 22 (sea cave), 26 (grotto), 27 (sea cave), 76, 85
Samoa, Apolima Island	pages 5, 24
Samoa, Manono Island	pages 40 (native lowland forest), 91
Samoa, Savaii Island	pages 14, 18–19, 23, 31, 33, 50–51, 78
Samoa, Upolu Island	pages 8, 15, 36, 38 (native coastal forest), 39, (native upland rainforest), 63, 64, 65, 74, 79, 80 & 81 (hurricane damage), 93, 97

Southern Pacific Ocean	pages 10, 11, 12, 13
Tokelau, Atafu Atoll	page 30
Tokelau, Faka'ofo Atoll	pages 1 (ship landing), 58, 62, 70–71
Tokelau, Nukunonu atoll	pages 44 (introduced food plants), 83
Tokelau, Teafua Tanu Island	pages 2, 6–7
Tonga, Tongatapu Island	pages 72, 94

Text Citations

[4] Mark Twain, *Roughing It in the Sandwich Islands*. (Honolulu: Mutual Publishing, First Thus Edition, 1994).

[17] "Duke Kahanamoku." donch.com. http://www.donch.com/lulhduke.htm.

[32] Traditional Hawaiian chant, from Marjorie Sinclair, *The Path of the Ocean: Traditional Poetry of Polynesia*. (Honolulu: University of Hawaii Press, 1982; Open Access Edition, 2019).

[49] Kauraka Kauraka, "Three Coconuts," *Dreams of a Rainbow*. (Rarotonga: W Publications, 1987).

[69] 'Epeli Hau'ofa, "Our Sea of Islands," from *The Contemporary Pacific*, Volume 6, Number 1: 147–61, 1994.

[84] Preamble to the National Climate Change Policy Framework Government of the Republic of the Marshall Islands, Majuro, 2011.

[101] Katharine Luomala, *Voices on the Wind: Polynesian Myths and Chants*. (Honolulu: Bishop Museum Press, 1992).

Polynesia

Published by Shanti Arts Publishing

Interior and cover design
by Shanti Arts Designs

Photographs by David Zurick and used with his permission

Shanti Arts LLC
193 Hillside Road
Brunswick, Maine 04011

www.shantiarts.com

Printed in the United States of America

ISBN: 978-1-956056-24-2 (softcover)

LCCN: 2021952577

Biographies

David Zurick is the author of numerous nonfiction and photography books. His books have won the National Outdoor Book Award, Banff Mountain Book Finalist Award, and Nautilus Award (for *Morning Coffee at the Goldfish Pond*, Shanti Arts). He is a Fellow of the Explorers Club and a recipient of the Mount Everest Award.

Alan Marcus is Professor and Chair of Film and Visual Culture, University of Aberdeen, Scotland, and an acclaimed filmmaker.

www.ingramcontent.com/pod-product-compliance
Lightning Source LLC
LaVergne TN
LVHW070129110826
845147LV00002B/219

* 9 7 8 1 9 5 6 0 5 6 2 4 2 *